THE STIMSON LEGACY

Architecture

in the

Urban West

LAWRENCE
KREISMAN

The Stimson Legacy: Architecture in the Urban West
Copyright © 1992 by Lawrence Kreisman

Published by
Willows Press
1204 Minor Avenue
Seattle, Washington 98101

Distributed by
University of Washington Press
P.O. Box 50096
Seattle, Washington 98145

ISBN 0-9631630-0-0 Hardcover;
0-9631630-1-9 Paperbound
Library of Congress catalogue card no. 91-068426
Designed by Virginia Hand
Printed by Dynagraphics, Inc.

Front cover photos, from top to bottom:
Multi-colored plaster ornament, Frederick Stimson ballroom, Seattle. Greg Gilbert
Thomas Douglas Stimson's Los Angeles residence on South Figueroa Street.
Lawrence Kreisman
The barrel-vaulted entrance foyer at the Charles Douglas Stimson residence, Seattle.
Greg Gilbert

Back cover photos, from top to bottom:
Terra cotta niche with bracket and urn ornamentation on the Coliseum Theatre facade.
Greg Gilbert
The Olympic Hotel under construction adjacent to the Metropolitan Theatre, 1924.
Pemco Webster and Stevens Collection, Museum of History and Industry
The garden approach to Norcliffe, the C.D. Stimson residence in the Highlands.
Mary Randlett

Background:
Brownline print of B. Marcus Priteca's elevation drawing for the Coliseum Theatre.
Collection of Thomas Stimson Bayley

FOREWORD

MARY RANDLETT

Dear Reader,

I hope you will find pleasure in getting to know my grandparents, Harriet and C.D. Stimson—their determination to create beautiful and liveable surroundings for their extended family, their devotion to their adopted community, their insistence on quality, their civility.

Seven grandchildren and six Stimson cousins were raised in Seattle, as were most of our children. Five of us were born at Norcliffe, our grandparents' home and the site of all our Sunday morning breakfasts and countless vacations.

At age four I sat atop the plough horse that prepared the rhododendron garden at Norcliffe. The courtyard in summer was fragrant with heliotrope, and orange trees in wooden tubs. I remember dominoes and parcheesi, hundreds of books, piano music, and a white polar bear rug with big teeth. I remember the smell of leather, pipe tobacco, firewood, big dogs in wet grass. I remember the taste of finnan haddie, fresh home-grown peas, prune whip, canteloupe ice cream at picnics, and cambric tea with honey. I read *Gone with the Wind* in front of the fire in the "blue room." Grandfather told great tales and took me for rides in his red roadster, in which he managed both steering wheel and stick shift while smoking a cigar and tipping his hat to passing ladies—all with only his one arm. Grandmother was ever-present and attentive for comfort, outings, or games.

As you read about the houses, office buildings, and theatres described here, please imagine the wonderful web of lives woven therein and the myriad individuals who worked on them and in them. They were new here, recently come from foreign lands—Germany, France, Armenia, Japan, Norway—and from elsewhere in America—Minnesota, Ohio, Illinois, Kentucky, New York. Together, these people created the character of the growing west by planting here, with pitched roofs, gables, and colored tiles, all that they cherished in memory from their places of origin.

We are heirs to a rich treasury of architectural forms from many homelands, adapted to this land. So was created a lively new culture, the urban American West.

The Stimson Legacy uses one family's ventures to illustrate how buildings were designed and made during the extraordinary era that ended in 1929. You will surely enjoy Greg Gilbert's beautiful color photographs, Mary Randlett's skilled reproductions of old snapshots and new color work, and Virginia Hand's attractive presentation. Especially you will appreciate, as I do, the fine research, respect for history, and painstaking care that Lawrence Kreisman has invested in this book.

I am happy to dedicate this book with gratitude and in loving memory to Harriet Mary Overton and Charles Douglas Stimson.

Priscilla Bullitt Collins

ACKNOWLEDGMENTS

The idea for this book developed from an article I wrote for *Pacific*, the Seattle Times Magazine, in 1989 in which letters from Kirtland Cutter to the Stimson family describe the working relationship between architect and client in the construction of a turn-of-the-century Seattle mansion. When family photographs, correspondence, and archival documents came to light on the death of Dorothy Stimson Bullitt, daughter of C.D. and Harriet Stimson, it became clear that the Stimson family had a more than passing interest in buildings. Along with their principal timber industry interests, real estate and urban development were threads that carried through several generations of this family in Chicago, Illinois, Los Angeles, California, and Seattle and Bellingham, Washington.

This publication is a synthesis of information drawn from interviews with family members and resources in private and public collections in the midwest and west coast. The author wishes to acknowledge and thank Thomas Stimson Bayley for access to photograph albums and property records at the Stimson Mill Company offices in Seattle; the staff of Manuscripts and University Archives Division, University of Washington Libraries, for access to the major repository of Stimson Mill Company records, including letterpress books and correspondence; Richard Engeman, Special Collections Division, University of Washington Libraries, for assistance with architectural drawings and architect files; Carolyn Marr and Richard Caldwell, Museum of History and Industry Library, for access to the Webster and Stevens Photograph Collection; and Brita Wendell of the Stimson Timber Company, who located photographs first published in *The Builder's Spirit*. The staff at the Los Angeles Public Library, the Commission on Chicago Landmarks, and the Chicago Historical Society, were also helpful in locating appropriate images. Mary Randlett prepared countless copy negatives and new prints from historic photographs. She, along with Greg Gilbert, took new color images of extant properties. Edward Nolan, former archivist at the Eastern Washington Historical Society, permitted copying of the Kirtland Cutter drawings from this institution's noteworthy collection. Galen Biery provided photographs of Bellingham buildings from his personal collection.

Readers who provided valuable comment on the manuscript were Dennis Andersen, Priscilla Collins, Stimson Bullitt, Thomas Stimson Bayley, Frank Bayley, and Wayne T. Dodge. Dawson Associates edited it with an eye to its organization and clarity. Graphic designer Virginia Hand, with whom I have worked on three previous publications, listened to my wish list and worked cooperatively at every stage to produce a book that allows the words and pictures to weave a story that is both informative and colorful.

Finally, Priscilla Collins, granddaughter of C.D. Stimson and the owner of the Stimson-Green Mansion, has been the kind of client a writer frequently dreams about but rarely experiences. From the inception of this project, she has been supportive of the concept and excited by the surprise discoveries made during research. As the scope and content of this book expanded over the course of two years of research and development, she encouraged it to grow as it needed to and to be the best that it could be.

CONTENTS

PREFACE

*F*or many of us, history has always been taught in terms of social, economic, and political actions and reactions. But history can be taught equally well by examining the types of buildings a society builds at particular periods. In fact, a culture's architecture—the materials used and the degree to which its buildings reflect social standing, technological advances, design influences, and popular taste—can tell us a great deal about a culture and can, in fact, be as reliable an indicator of a society's development as more typical approaches.

All cultures build. What and how it builds indicates its access to and skill in using local or not so local natural resources and simple or sophisticated approaches to structure, function, and decoration. Buildings and their ornament can serve strictly utilitarian purposes or they can be embellished, based upon contemporary belief systems, religious values, or foreign influence and traditions. They can be designed for the worship or use of a whole community or simply for the whim and ego of one individual. The built world is a record of our history.

This book examines the commercial and residential buildings constructed by members of one American family over the course of a century to explain changing taste in American society— and particularly in the development of an urban west. The Stimson family was certainly a fortunate one in terms of its financial successes and therefore was able to build structures of some significance. This family's accomplishments are important as they reflect a common thread of human nature—the need to provide a legacy, to make a statement to the immediate world and to have done some things for the improvement of that world.

Four generations in the Stimson family are traced from the forests of Michigan in the 1840s to Chicago in the 1880s, Los Angeles in the 1890s, and Seattle and Bellingham, Washington, until 1930. While family descendants continue to contribute substantially to Northwest social, cultural, and political life, and have, in fact, been involved in urban development, these later generations are not "builders" to the extent of those before them and are therefore not discussed at great length.

The Stimsons' contribution to public and private architecture was not on the order of the Vanderbilts, the Carnegies, or the Rockefellers. Rather, it reflects the commonly felt urge of American society to build comfortable and stylish homes. It also demonstrates the interest in real estate investment that stimulated development of office buildings, hotels, and theatres in major cities. Ultimately, the cities of the west were settled and built by self-made men and women whose interest was motivated partly by financial gain, partly by wish for recognition and acceptance by peers, and partly by altruism and the desire to do good deeds and to build new communities.

In the history of westward expansion, certain names appear in each generation in connection with certain industries. The strongly held familial obligations to hold on to and build upon the family business and pass it on to a new generation is evidenced in all business, whether that might be the small dry goods store that becomes a major department store or a fledgling boat business that grows into a huge shipyard. The phenomenon is especially apparent in the mining, manufacturing, railroad, and timber industries of 19th and 20th century America.

The evolution of lumber dynasties coincides with the exploitation of resources from the Atlantic to the Pacific coast. As a rule, these families followed the evergreen forests, beginning in Maine—the "Pine Tree State" —then travelling west to the vast timber regions surrounding the Great Lakes in Michigan, Wisconsin, and Minnesota, and finally going across the Rockies to the gigantic forests of Washington, Oregon, and California.

In the Pacific Northwest, several families established and maintained lumber dynasties. Often, because they met in the same social and business circles, members of these families intermarried and combined holdings. Sometimes, as was the case with the Stimsons, estates were divided among family members so that some had control of lumber and mill interests while others inherited real estate, and stocks and bonds.

Their major business might have been in lumber and milling, but it was typical for such men to diversify their holdings, becoming active participants in real estate development, railroading, and industry. As the "movers and shakers" of their time, they also took leadership roles in civic affairs and social causes. Their wives, blessed with the leisure time to devote to worthy efforts, and brought up with an appreciation of music, arts, and theatre, generally attempted to fill the gaps in culture and education that were glaringly apparent in a young city like Seattle.

Among these pioneer lumbermen, few stood higher in financial or social circles than the Stimson family. Thomas Douglas Stimson and four of his children, Charles Douglas and Frederick of Seattle and, to a lesser extent, Willard and Ezra of Los Angeles, collectively provided a bold legacy of buildings that expressed an optimistic view of the growth of western cities and strongly held beliefs about the importance of family life and the home as gathering place for extended family.

The story of the Stimsons and their impact upon urban architecture, popular taste, and cultural endeavors is a case study to describe how, in fact, western cities shed their early-day images of dirt streets and white clapboard cottages and slipped awkwardly but with great anticipation and excitement into the twentieth century American urban experience.

Thomas Douglas (T.D.) Stimson,
1866. Stimson Mill Company
(SMC)

"Giant firs along government road
that are the wonder of Eastern
tourists." Caption from Stimson
family scrapbook.

TIMBER

MICHIGAN ROOTS

Thomas Douglas Stimson was born in French Mills (now Fort Covington), New York, in July, 1827, to Horace and Julia Douglas Stimson. His mother died soon after, and the family moved to Van Buren County in Michigan. An excerpt from an 1880 publication, *History of Berrien and Van Buren Counties*, says of Horace Stimson:

> Horace Stimson, who became distinguished as the first post-master at Lawrence, moved from Kalamazoo to Section One in Lawrence, in 1836. Orrin Sutton built a double log house for Stimson, and finished it just in time to be used for the first town meeting held April 3, 1837.[1]

With Horace Stimson's log cabin began a remarkable legacy of buildings built expressly by and for that family for generations in the west. Here too began the long tradition of ties between the personal lives of the Stimson family and life in the broader civic and social community which they shared.

---

1. Thomas Stimson Bayley, *The Stimson Family* (Seattle, Washington: Ballard Printing and Publishing, 1976), 1.

Letterhead, T.D. Stimson Big Rapids
offices, 1879. SMC

Because of friction between Thomas Douglas and his father's new wife, T.D. left home at fourteen and found work driving oxen at a lumber camp on the Muskegon River in Michigan. This was an era of timber cutting and lumber milling on a remarkable scale in Wisconsin, Illinois, and Michigan. The forests of Maine and the northeast were rapidly being depleted and lumber men were excited by the forests of the Great Lakes area. Muskegon was fast developing into a forest products center because of its ample natural harbor and its accessibility to the densely forested valley through which the Muskegon River flowed.

An intrepid and adventurous man accustomed to hard work, T.D. (as he was commonly referred to all his life) partnered with Delos Blodgett, the foreman of the woods crew at the logging camp. The two of them explored the dense pine forest in the north country (now Clare County). They bought the tract from the government and established a lumber camp—the first lumbering operation on the Muskegon above Big Rapids. In the following years, they expanded operations and made significant profits. As timber lands to the south were exhausted, the lands in which Stimson and Blodgett had invested increased greatly in value. The financial fortunes of these men multiplied rapidly. T.D. gained a reputation for enterprise and integrity which was to remain with him throughout his life.

On September 28, 1853, T.D. Stimson married Achsah Jane Spencer in Grand Rapids. She was the daughter of Blodgett's aunt and uncle, also frontier loggers. For the first few months of their married life, the couple lived in a one-room farm house in Croton, a tiny village on the Muskegon. Freight teamsters driving back and forth between Muskegon and Big Rapids often stopped at the little house overnight, giving the couple little privacy. Grandson Charles Willard (C.W.) Stimson once asked his grandmother what present his grandfather had given her that had meant the most to her. She replied without hesitation that it was "when he put a partition up in our house at Croton."[2]

They moved to a nearby farm and, in 1858, the growing family moved to another farm, this one adjoining Mercosta County about four miles north of Big Rapids. During this time, T.D. began operating his own mill, and within a year built a large new house just south of his former one outside Big Rapids. That town was a "very small clearing in the woods" with fifteen or twenty people. The Muskegon River at Big Rapids was unbridged when Thomas Lazell came to build the house for T.D. in 1860. He crossed in a

2. John R. Ross, *The Builder's Spirit: The History of Stimson Lumber Company* (Portland: John Ross and Associates, 1983), viii.

canoe.[3] The Stimsons had six children: Willard Horace born in 1854, Olive Jane in 1855, Charles Douglas in 1857, Ezra Thomas in 1860, Frederick Spencer in 1867, and J.D. in 1870. The boys were always called by their initials; in fact J.D. was given only his initials at birth and later adopted the name Jay.

T.D. sold the mill, his new house, goods and stock in 1863 to invest in an oil venture in Canada. It quickly soured, leaving him virtually penniless. Undaunted, he returned to Muskegon and contracted to locate and buy government timberlands with funds supplied by the Ryerson Lumber Company. Martin Ryerson was a prominent lumberman and entrepreneur in Chicago, and he and Stimson split the stock equally. Stimson's success in this venture provided the money he needed for a second start on his own. And his business relationship with Martin Ryerson led to a friendship which would, in Chicago twenty years later, lead him into real estate interests and an ultimate shift in emphasis from timber to buildings.

T.D. Stimson was altogether a born woodsman. He is described reverently in family accounts as a tireless worker with a saving sense of humor, who was never dismayed by hardships or obstacles. He seemed, in fact, to thrive on them. Not until much later in his life did he begin to delegate work —and then only to his own family and to a small handful of long-time, trusted mill hands. This practice was one of the principal factors in his ongoing success.

During the 1870s, T.D. greatly expanded his timber and milling operations. In 1873, he incorporated the Stimson, Clark Manufacturing Company in Big Rapids with himself as president; J.J. Fay, Jr., his sister Olive's husband, as secretary; and his brother Willard (W.H.) as managing director. Stimson built a large new mill in Big Rapids and, along with it, a well-equipped window sash and planing mill to accommodate the lucrative house-building market in the Midwest. In 1877, he had a palatial house built for his family in Big Rapids. It was constructed at a cost of over $30,000 and with the intention that it would be the family's permanent home.

The 1870s was a period of excess and exuberance in architecture for those who could afford it. From their humble prairie roots, those self-made men with their millions sought to have their homes reflect and announce to the community that they had indeed "made it." The Stimson house in Big Rapids was typical. Located on a prime corner lot, it was an Empire style

Stimson's French Empire house in Big Rapids, ca. 1882. SMC

---

3. Ross, 4.

Charles Douglas (C.D.) Stimson at 16 years of age, 1873. SMC

mansion that actually rose three floors, its third floor somewhat disguised by a mansard roof punctuated with ornately framed dormers A mansard tower with a widow's walk crowned the central pavilion and raised the height of the edifice an additional floor. The towered form would reappear in later Stimson houses.

The two principal floors had high-ceilinged rooms and angled bays that would have let in much light, had the period not been one devoted to privacy, to multiple layers of draperies and curtains and shades to keep out the sun with its harmful effects on the furniture fabrics and fine complexions. The physical comfort and prosperity reflected by this environment would have an impact upon twenty-year-old Charles, seventeen-year-old Ezra, and ten-year-old Frederick and shape their definitions of "home" in the years to come.

Charles Douglas (C.D.) attended a boarding school affiliated with the University of Notre Dame in Indiana for two years, then entered public schools in Grand Rapids. He was a highly energetic boy with an abounding degree of self-confidence which was put to its test when he developed an infection in his right arm that ultimately required amputation. His parents, and particularly his mother, did little to pamper his condition. Instead, she expected him to do all those things he had done prior to the loss. He engaged in all kinds of sports and activities and, in the process, developed his left arm and hand to an amazing dexterity and strength.

T.D. was a hard taskmaster. He had grown up working for everything he got and he expected the same from his sons. They worked in the mill from an early age—at no pay. T.D. was not overly generous with his salaries either. C.D. left home rather than accept the twenty dollars a month his father offered him. He found work as a clerk for significantly more money and refused to return home until an agreement was reached. In it, T.D. gave him a planing mill and all the profits that he and his older brother W.H. could make out of it. This move established the sons firmly in the family lumber business. They began selling lumber in the Midwest and set up a headquarters in Cincinnati and later in Kansas City and Wichita.[4]

T.D. moved his operations from Big Rapids to Lakeside, then a suburb of Muskegon, in 1880. He built a second mill at Muskegon on what later became the site of the Continental Motor Company. In 1882 at Big Rapids, he witnessed the marriage of his son C.D. to Harriet Mary Overton, a fair-haired girl born in Adams, New York and educated to be a professional musician in Ann

4. Bayley, 9.

Arbor. The couple settled in Muskegon, where in 1884, their son Thomas Douglas, named by—and for—his grandfather, was born.

In the T.D. Stimson Company, in conjunction with his sons' mill, operated four steamers at that time: "Stafford," which shipped to Chicago, Milwaukee, and Muskegon; "R. Holland," which operated out of Marine City, between Lake St. Clair and Lake Huron; and "J.W. Westcott" and "T.D. Stimson," both of which operated out of Chicago. In the early 1880s, T.D. turned over his control of the older mill to his three eldest children.—W.H., C.D., and their sister Olive Stimson Fay and her husband, J.J. Fay, Jr. T.D. and his wife Achsah Jane then began deeding large tracts of timber land in Michigan and Minnesota to their sons.[5]

Water Street, Chicago River east from State Street, 1889. Chicago Historical Society (CHS)

CHICAGO

The young men operated the mill for a few years until 1886, when C.D. decided to join his father in Chicago. T.D. had set up his headquarters in an office there at 244 South Water Street, and C.D. supervised the lumber yard in South Chicago. Frederick left his studies at Swarthmore College to help out in Chicago until he was sent in 1887 to manage shipping at the Muskegon facility. During these years, attempting to find new sources and outlets for lumber, the family had opened a lumberyard in Atkinson, Nebraska, run by Ezra; bought timber in Traverse City, Michigan; and built a lumber and shingle mill run by Olive and her husband J.J. Fay, Jr.,

T. D. STIMSON,
MANUFACTURER AND DEALER
LUMBER, LATH & SHINGLES,
238 SOUTH WATER ST.
MILLS:
MUSKEGON, MICH.   CHICAGO, ILL., 10-18 188 6

Letterhead, Stimson Chicago offices, 1886. SMC

5. Bayley, 11.

Architect George Edbrooke's residence at 3314-16 S. Calumet Avenue in its present condition. Bob Thall, Commission on Chicago Landmarks (CCL)

Far right, T.D. Stimson's residence at 3132 S. Calumet Avenue showing present condition. Bob Thall, CCL

T.D. had also bought a house at 3132 Calumet Avenue, a prestigious neighborhood comparable to Prairie Avenue in the number of lumber barons, meatpackers, bankers, and retailers who lived there. In keeping with his millionaire neighbors' homes, his townhouse was an imposing stone building designed by local architect George H. Edbrooke (ca. 1845-1894).

Edbrooke was the son of a builder in Chicago and brother of Willoughby J. Edbrooke, an architect whose successes would overshadow his brother's for much of his life.[6] George Edbrooke did commercial work in his native city and in Detroit (American Building, 1887) and St. Louis (Commercial Building, 1887). He was frequently called upon to do residences in newly developing middle-class and upper-class neighborhoods. In 1889, he left Chicago and established an office in New York. His most important work, the Brooklyn Savings Bank, was under construction at the time of his death by suicide in February,1894.

In 1884, Edbrooke designed his own three-story residence at 3316 South Calumet Avenue in the Douglas neighborhood—an area first developed by Senator Stephen A. Douglas and which, between 1880 and 1900, established itself as a distinguished enclave for upper-income residents. Because the majority of its homeowners were professionals, capitalists, and executives of a variety of business enterprises, the neighborhood was well supplied with architect-designed townhouses. The firm of Adler and Sullivan, for example, had built approximately fifteen houses in the immediate vicinity prior to their commission to design the Auditorium Theatre and Hotel building in 1886.[7]

Edbrooke's residence was built of Joliet limestone. It com-

6. From the commencement of his practice in 1867 through the 1880s, Willoughby's commissions were substantial and far-reaching. Along with his Chicago work, he designed the Georgia State Capitol; opera houses in Denver, Colorado and Dubuque, Iowa; the campus of Notre Dame college; and churches and public buildings throughout the Midwest. He was also supervising architect for the U.S. Treasury Building. *The Building Budget* (Chicago: October 31, 1887)118; Henry F. Withey, A.I.A. and Elsie Rathburn Withey, *Biographical Dictionary of American Architects (Deceased)* (Los Angeles: 1970),189; *Bernham Index of American Architectural Literature.*

7. *Douglas Historic District Prelimary Summary of Information*, Commission on Chicago Historical and Architectural Landmarks, February, 1987, and National Register of Historic Places Inventory and Nomination form for the Douglas Historic District.

bined Flemish stepped gables with a Romanesque entrance portal guarded by carved serpents, an oriel bay projecting from the second-floor corner, and colorful, stained glass transoms. Either at the same time or shortly thereafter, he used the identical design in an abbreviated form without a north wing and entrance, for property he owned at 3132 South Calamut Avenue. It was this house at 3132 South Calumet—so different in scale and style to the large, free-standing dwelling common a decade or two earlier—that T.D. Stimson purchased when he moved to Chicago. Shortly after the purchase in October, 1886 a permit was issued for alterations to the house and for the building of a two-story barn 45 feet by 25 feet on the property to house his carriage and horses.[8]

In the short time during which T.D. resided in the city (1886-1891) he made real estate investments in and around the Chicago area. This was the first time that T.D. had put large amounts of excess capital into land other than timber tracts, and it proved to be a successful buffer against the occasionally fluctuating profits of the mills. Fellow lumberman Martin Ryerson and a small circle of business associates influenced T.D. to invest in commercial real estate. While he held some small commercial properties in Big

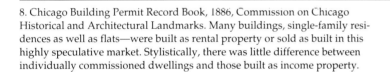

8. Chicago Building Permit Record Book, 1886, Commission on Chicago Historical and Architectural Landmarks. Many buildings, single-family residences as well as flats—were built as rental property or sold as built in this highly speculative market. Stylistically, there was little difference between individually commissioned dwellings and those built as income property.

Below, Auditorium Building (Adler and Sullivan) nearing completion, 1890. CCL

Rapids and Muskegon, Michigan, and had chosen to reside in substantial homes in Big Rapids and on Calumet Avenue in Chicago, he had to this point been primarily an owner of forestland—not urban real estate.

In Stimson's retirement years, his Chicago associations led him with some passion and sense of urgency into the real estate and building development field. Between 1889 and 1891, he purchased many thousands of dollars in stock certificates in the Adler and Sullivan designed Auditorium Building, the Burnham and Root designed Rookery, and the Baumann and Huehl designed Chamber of Commerce Building. He also purchased several commercial properties in Chicago.[9]

A logging road cuts through the giant evergreen forests of a government tract, 1910. From Stimson family scrapbook.

WASHINGTON TERRITORY

In 1884, the family recognized that standing timber in the Midwest, at the rate at which it was being cut, would soon be depleted, as it had been in the Northeast. T.D. hired James Roe to conduct a thorough survey of standing timber districts in the south, in California, and in the Northwest. During the next four years, C.D. and W.H. investigated these tracts and found most of them unsuitable except for Puget Sound in Washington Territory. T.D. joined James Roe and together they returned to the Midwest with glowing reports of the seemingly unlimited timber resources of the northwest corner—it was indeed a lumberman's paradise and an all but untapped one.[10]

The *San Francisco Chronicle*, like most contemporary tabloids looking to boost the west coast and its potential, reported that standing timber in Washington would amount to "413,000,000,000 feet, or a solid train 15,000 feet of lumber to the car stretching 154,000 miles or 6 times around the earth and enough cars left to make a train stretching from Tacoma across the continent to the middle of the Atlantic."

---

9. Letterpress books, 1889-1891, Stimson Mill Company Records, University of Washington Libraries, Seattle. These properties were on Wabash Avenue, on South Park Avenue and 71st Street, Halsted Street, Wentworth Avenue, and, jointly with Ryerson, a house on Fourney Street.

10. Bayley, 13.

Although there were lumber operations in the Pacific Northwest well before Stimson moved there, many mills were struggling to survive under less than optimal conditions. Henry Yesler's steam-powered sawmill was established in Seattle in 1853 shortly after the early settlers retreated from inhospitable Alki Point to the relative calm of Elliott Bay. That same year, the Meigs Mill at Port Madison and the Renton and Terry mill at Port Orchard, were destroyed by fire. They were rebuilt but burned again in 1864 and 1869, respectively. The Port Blakely Mill Company was destroyed in 1888 and rebuilt to become the largest in the world before it burned to the ground in 1907. A mill in West Seattle began operating in 1864 and burned in 1867. The rebuilt mill burned too. In 1875, Mr. Colman built a mill which burned in 1879, was rebuilt in 1881, and eventually burned again. With such a volatile history, it is said that T.D. told his sons, "Boys, you'd better get out there pretty quick before they burn up the whole dang country."

C.D., Harriet, and 4-year-old Thomas left for Puget Sound in the fall of 1888, to be followed shortly by W.H., his wife Kate, and their son Charles Willard (C.W.). Their father had plans for C.D.

James Roe helped Stimson determine the best location for timber on the west coast. SMC

Northwest timber camp in Snohomish County near Marysville, ca 1895. Dorothy Stimson Bullitt Archives (DSB)

Yesler Avenue (Way) looking east,
Seattle, ca. 1888. DSB

Frederick Stimson, ca. 1880 SMC

and F.S. to run the mill in Washington and for W.H. and E.T. to market the lumber in Oregon and California, which is the way things ultimately evolved.[11]

C.D. used to remark on how trifles sometimes determine crucially important decisions. In the Pullman car coming west, the gentleman seated opposite the Stimsons engaged C.D. in conversation. C.D. said, in reply to the other's inquiry, that he was enroute to Puget Sound. The man thereupon observed that "of course" he meant by that Tacoma. "Not necessarily", replied C.D. But the man persisted so vehemently in his boosting of Tacoma as the only city on the Sound. He insisted so arrogantly, in fact, that the longer he pressed the more determined C.D. became that Tacoma was decidedly not the place where he would settle. Instead, on their arrival in Tacoma, they boarded the steamer "Olympian" and disembarked in Seattle on February 5, 1889.[12]

The family settled into an apartment at the Griffith House on Second Avenue and Pike Street, where they lived for half a year. With an eye to investigating all potential sites for a mill, C.D. made numerous trips to explore the resources from Olympia north to Bellingham. In the early spring, on the suggestion of Captain W.R.

---

11. Bayley, 14.

12. Ibid.

Ballard, Stimson bought a dilapidated mill at Salmon Bay and turned it into one of Ballard's most important businesses.

In April of that year, the Stimson Land Company was incorporated to carry on "a general logging and lumbering business in Washington Territory; the building, buying, leasing and operating of one or more saw mills; the cutting, hauling, and booming of saw logs and piles; the manufacture of doors, window sash-frames and blinds; the cutting of laths and shingles and the doing of every other thing in the sale or manufacture of lumber, logs, and piles; construct railroads, build flumes or canals; to build, buy or own steamboats and sailing vessels and to purchase, hold, mortgage, sell and convey real and personal property."[13]

The Stimsons were all directors—Thomas Douglas, Willard Horace, Ezra Thomas, Charles Douglas, and Frederick Spencer. T.D. was president, with C.D. treasurer and W.H. secretary. W.H. soon bought nearly 40,000 acres in Washington and Oregon for the company in addition to vast tracts that members of the family bought on their own.[14] The Stimson Mill Company was incorporated on January 13, 1890 and T.D. was elected president of the board. W.H. was vice president, E.T. secretary, and C.D. treasurer and general manager of the mill.

On November 27, 1891, T.D. wrote to his sons:

Dear boys,

I have been to Oshkosh and just returned this morning. Bought of Challoner two ten blockers, knot saws, and all machinery including shafting and pulleys for the upper floors to your mill. I think I have bought all of the machinery you will now want in the shingle mill and think you had better set the machines 20 feet apart. I want you to send me a sketch made by the millwright showing the location of the engine, size of the drive wheel, location and size of

20th Avenue East looking north, Ballard, DSB.

C.D. Stimson, 1886. SMC

13. Bayley, 16.

14. Bayley, 17.

Stimson Mill Company engraved letterhead ca. 1895.

the main counterline or lower floor. If you haven't bought this latter main counterline and pulleys that are necessary for main shaft, I will buy it here of Challoners and ship it with the stuff in same car.

Stimson also purchased shingle machines from that firm and four kiln buildings from the Independent Dryer Company of Chicago. A note from "Charlie" to his father on April 30, 1891 says, "Started up the sawmill this morning, now we are running the saw mill with one board saw in the shingle mill and it all runs very nicely; made 235,000 shingles yesterday. The log slide in the old mill works all right and we have at present plenty of orders."[15]

With the decision to settle in Seattle, C.D. and his brothers

15. Incoming correspondence file, 1891, Stimson Mill Company Records, University of Washington Libraries.

C.D. Stimson Residence,
(foreground left of center) First
Avenue No. and Ward Street, ca.
1895. SMC

Frederick and Willard all planned to provide their families with comfortable homes. In March, 1889, C.D. began construction on a new house at the corner of Ward Street and First Avenue North on the south slope of Queen Anne Hill. By June, it was nearly completed. His offices in the Newland Block on Columbia Street between Second and Third Avenues had miraculously escaped damage during the Seattle Fire of 1889; they rapidly filled with other less fortunate businessmen with whom C.D. shared space. As he was crowded in on all sides, he decided to move to the new house even before it was finished, living in the attic while carpenters finished the main floors. He and Harriet and Thomas lived there for twelve years. In 1892, a daughter Dorothy Frances was born there. It was from this house that C.D. saddled his horse, put his lunch in a saddlebag, and rode over the top of the hill and down into Ballard each morning to his offices at the mill.[16]

The comfortably large three-story house stood on a corner

16. Bayley, p.16.

lot. Substantial by Seattle standards, it was in no way comparable to the elaborate Yesler and Colman homes in the downtown area or the distinctive towered mansion George Kinnear had built nearby in 1886-87, which was noted for its landscaped grounds and fountains.

The architecture of C.D.'s house was typical of the popular Queen Anne style in which most ambitious houses were built during that period. Its assymetry and idiosyncratic form was evocative of a romantic heritage. The half-timbered elements of the Stimson house faintly echoed English medieval houses. It had two-story bays, ample gables and porches, and its share of decorative shingles in the skirting separating the first and second floor bays and in the crowns of its gable ends. From its site, views of the city and Elliott Bay opened up to the south and west. While lower down on the hill housing was starting to fill the lots, numerous cleared sites still awaited builders.

Dorothy and Thomas Stimson in the yard of the Ward Street residence, ca, 1895. DSB

Frederick selected a lot just uphill of C.D. at 128 Aloha Street for a fourteen-room three-story Queen Anne-style house. He had it built in the spring and summer of 1891 for an estimated cost of $4,900. On July 27, 1891, he wrote his father, "We are nearly ready to go into our house. Will be moved and settled I hope by the 8th of next month. We are going to have a fine place." Its features included a pedimented entrance porch and wrap-around veranda, sawn decorative bargeboards, and a tower. Interior woodwork was in the Eastlake style, with open spindlework staircase balusters and screens in the stairhall. Gold embossed wall-papers with floral, fruit, and flower designs covered the walls.[17]

T.D. oversaw much of the early business in the Northwest. Beginning with his first trip to Puget Sound in 1888 with James Roe, T.D. frequently came up the coast by train from Los Angeles, his "retirement home," to chair the board meetings as his empire expanded heavily into Washington Territory. He purchased prop-

17. When the F.S. Stimsons moved to their West Highland Drive address, this house was sold to Solomon Rogers, a clothing merchant, and maintained with few alterations until the death in 1961 of Mrs. Eva Rogers. Karl Strandberg, a Seattle contractor, purchased the property and the house was demolished to make way for an apartment house. Original gaslight fixtures and gold embossed wallpaper were used in restoration of the Sylvester House (1857) in Olympia, according to a P.I. article.

erty from William Bailey in November of 1890 for his frequent stays in the city. Known as the Strawberry House, it was offered to F.S. and Nellie Stimson as an interim living place while they built their own home. They chose to live with C.D., and Strawberry House was put up for sale; while they waited for a buyer, the family rented it out at $20 a month.

On October 22, 1892, Frank Devendorf wrote from the Chicago office to T.D. Stimson in Los Angeles:

> I attended the opening of the World's Fair yesterday and saw the building that the Washington people are putting up. It is being built entirely of logs that have been contributed by the lumbermen of that state and is going to be a great attraction. I saw the name of the Stimson Mill Company on some of them. There are some sticks now in the building that are fully 125 feet long and about 4 feet square.[18]

It would have been a great source of pride for Stimson, now firmly grounded on the West Coast, to know that his lumber was representing the state at the World's Columbian Exposition in Chicago.

Below, Stimson Mill Company promotional photograph of 40 foot circumference log. DSB

18. Letterpress book, 1892, Stimson Mill Company Records.

Christmas gathering at Figueroa
Street with the entire family. T.D.
Stimson stands alone right of
center. DSB

Background, northeast corner of
Third and Hill Streets, Los
Angeles, ca. 1890. Los Angeles
Public Library (LAPL)

Chapter 2

Thomas Douglas Stimson in Los Angeles

Leaving the Calumet Avenue house in the charge of his daughter, Olive Fay, T.D. moved to Los Angeles in 1890 to retire to a healthier climate than Chicago. He found himself at a place and time where his money and business sense were needed and welcomed. He wrote his office manager, Frank Devendorf, "Am going to buy some property here—a home and some other property. We are all well. Weather fine. Peaches in bloom. Strawberries 15 ct. a box. I have got a nice team and the roads are good."[1]

Los Angeles in 1890 was in the midst of a depression. According to contemporary commentaries, nearly every industry was at a standstill "while capitalists held back, fearing to invest means where prospects were so gloomy and uncertain." It was only the influx of outsiders with ready cash and a willingness to invest in the local economy that stimulated growth. T. D. was just such a person. According to J. M. Guinn in his *Southern California: Historical and Biographical Record*, "It was then that his firm faith in the future of Los Angeles asserted itself. With an optimism born of a

---

1. Correspondence file, 1890, Stimson Mill Company Records.

Spring Street looking north from First. Opening day of the double track cable line, June 8, 1889. LAPL

far-seeing judgement, he gave himself to the development of local resources, furnished employment to many workmen, erected buildings of a most substantial character, and made improvements of permanent value to the city."[2]

THE PRIVATE REALM

Stimson selected a site only a short trolley ride south of the city, in the residential area along Figueroa Street at its intersection with West Adams Boulevard for his own 30 room mansion. On its completion in 1893, he and Achsah Jane invited the entire family to Christmas with them. The Stimson clan, by then totalling twenty one children and grandchildren, convened in Los Angeles for the first of what was to become a traditional family gathering. Before they had their own homes built in Los Angeles, Ezra and Annie and Willard and Kate Stimson shared the house with their parents. In later years, some of the city's wealthiest and most important families—among them oil millionaire Edward L. Doheny—would build homes in Chester Place, a private street directly adjoining the Stimson property.

T.D. had come from Chicago with set ideas about what made for a proper house. In that city, brick and stone were common materials and substantial medieval castles had been built on the Gold Coast, along Michigan Avenue's Mansion Row and North State Parkway area, the great stone townhouses along Grand Boulevard leading to Washington Park, Prairie Avenue, and his own exclusive Douglas neighborhood. He wanted one like that for himself—even if it was somewhat anachronistic in southern California—and went about finding an architect who could design one. In twenty-seven-year-old H. Carroll Brown he found a willing hand. Brown hailed from Champaign, Illinois and came to Los Angeles in the 1880s. His family homestead had been located at Eighth and Broadway. At the time of their acquaintence, Brown was a relatively unknown local

---

2. Gwinn, J. M. *Southern California: Historical and Biographical Record* , 231.

architect. There are no records of prior work. But Stimson's faith in him was rewarded.[3]

Brown designed a three-and-one-half story sandstone building in the popular Romanesque Style but with borrowings from northern Europe and England as well—a melding of various historically derived design elements ranging from Gothic and Neoclassical to Queen Anne. With its crenellated tower, an open balcony at the third floor supported by lacy scrolled corbels, and a distinctive Flemish gable with Palladian windows, the house attracted much local attention. The overall impact was that of solidity, permanency, and wealth.

While not the only house in Los Angeles to be modeled after a medieval castle, at a cost of $130,000 in 1891 dollars, it was the most expensive house ever built in the city to that time. While others built sprawling Queen Anne Victorian mansions of wood with decorated bargeboards, spindlework verandas, round and

Above, 2421 S. Figueroa Street front view, ca. 1895. LAPL

Below, Stimson's carriage and horses on the drive, Figueroa Street, ca. 1895. LAPL

3. A member of the Southern California Chapter of the American Institute of Architects, Brown kept offices in the Stimson Building for much of his career. Brown's reputation built with the Stimson projects, and he established a client list that allowed for a residence for Captain William Banning on Hoover Street, the Metropole Hotel at Avalon, and other local residential and commercial commissions. In his last years, he was noted for the design of the Puente High School. Obituary, *Southern Builder and Contractor*, November 26,1920; *Architect and Engineer*, Dec., 1920, 15; Whitey, *Biographical Dictionary*, 80.

Perspective of the Figueroa Street residence by Curro. DSB

square bays and shingled gables, Stimson's house would remind him of his recent sojourn in Chicago—as long as he didn't look out his window at the huge date palms fronting his property.

Some observers would think it strange that a man who had become a millionaire in the timber industry would build his house of stone. But such people were probably not privileged to venture inside. The interior was a woodsman's dream, with richly panelled walls and coffered and beamed ceilings in magnificent hardwoods—ash, sycamore, birch, mahogany, walnut, gumwood, and oak— with furnishings to match. Stimson had apparently struck a deal with the Pullman Company, which was building a specially equipped set of Pullman railcars for the 1893 World's Columbian Exposition in Chicago. Each car was to be outfitted with different woods. Stimson purchased enough of each kind to panel his new house.[4]

He also outfitted the house through his connections and frequent visits back to Chicago and the Midwest. It is unlikely he would have found the quality of goods he desired and to which he was accustomed in the Los Angeles area. And as his business routinely packed railroad cars and shipped goods, it would not be out of the ordinary for him. While H. Carroll Brown might have suggested interior features, it appears to have been Stimson himself who did the shopping and ordering. He gave the Carsley and East Manufacturing Company of Chicago the principal interior design contract with the understanding that Carl Willert, one of their chief designers, would be in charge.

Copies of letters written from the Stimson Mill Company Chicago office and letters from Carlsey and East during 1891-92 reveal the extent of these activities and provide a picture of what went into the decoration of the house.[5] Stimson was apparently so comfortable with the woodwork of his Chicago townhouse that he wanted to replicate it in his new home. On February 14, 1891, in response to an inquiry by Stimson from Los Angeles, his mill supervisor Frank Devendorf responded:

> In regard to your bookcase mantel and sideboard, I have telephoned up to the Frost Manufacturing Company today and they

---

4. Bayley, p. 20.

5. Excerpts are drawn from correspondence in the Stimson Mill Company Records, 1891-1892.

say they don't preserve the drawings this length of time. Probably the cheapest way is to have photographs taken of them. Frost would like to duplicate these and ship them to you and thinks he could save you money. If you want prices on the work I can get them and write you.

During March and April a photographer did indeed document the interiors, although the darkness of the interiors made the job a difficult one. T.D. was sent photographs of the hall, the library showing stairway and pillars, and the sideboard on April 7; on April 10, a photograph of the fireplace in the dining room was sent.

Brown was meanwhile having problems finding enough good quality stone in the size and quantity he needed to build the house as he wanted. After visiting the Lordsburg quarry, he wrote in disgust to T.D. Stimson on May 26, 1891:

I am utterly discouraged as to getting the dimension stone we will want for window heads and sills for your residence from the Lordsburg quarry...little progress had been made in getting through the shattered and seamed rock to the longer and more solid rock that lies further in the mountain...It will be a squeeze to get enough larger stone for the water table and window heads and sills for foundation and that may take a month yet. All the other stone for the foundation is on the building site and cut ready to lay up...I don't think it advisable to lay up the veranda walls at present even though we had the large stone, as they would be in the way when we come to build the main walls of the house...I wish you would talk to Mrs. S. as to the advisability of changing the trimmings of house (which includes all the large stone) to the "San Fernando" buff stone. I think it would be much more satisfactory and look exceedingly well. This stone can be obtained in any size or length and it is one of the best stones both in color and durability in the State.

T.D. Stimson with bowler hat and cane, at a southern California resort hotel, ca. 1890. SMC

The Stimsons evidently took a "wait and see" attitude to his request. On July 19, Brown wrote again:

The more I think of it, the more I am persuaded that we will be compelled to change the stone in the superstructure of your residence. We have at last succeeded in getting enough large stone for the basement window caps, but we will both be in our graves before there are enough more large stones taken from the Lordsburg quarry to finish the house as I have designed it and to change the design to fit the stone we can get would take too long a time and utterly ruin it. I am so well pleased with the effect of this stone when laid up in a mass that I am very loath to abandon it altogether and therefore would suggest that we use it for the body of the work and for all trimmings use the buff San Fernando stone. It would make a beautiful combination and I am sure you and Mrs. Stimson would like it exceedingly well when it was completed.

The Stimsons decided in favor of this plan, and the house was completed with rough-cut Lordsburg stone and the lighter San Fernando sandstone for lintels, sills, balconies, balustrades, and the crown trim of the tower and stepped gables.

By June 20th, 1891, a contract with Carsley and East Manufacturing Company in Chicago had been forwarded for T.D.'s inspection, along with a copy of the specifications for the Los Angeles house. Building progressed through the summer, fall and winter. Economy was considered throughout so long as it did not compromise the design. As an example, his foreman E.D. Elliott wrote to T.D. on September 30, 1891 with the prices for both black and green slate, the latter being less expensive. "The dust will certainly cover the slate so that it would be impossible to tell what the color is. Have consulted with Mrs. Stimson and she is not opposed to it."

By the following spring, materials were still being sent west to complete the house. On April 30, 1892, Mr. W. H. Allen, Stimson's Los Angeles manager of the house project, was informed that Carsley Manufacturing Company had been given a check for $5,000 on account of the residence contract. On May 3rd, T.D. wrote to the James H. Rice Co. "I accept your proposition...You may ship the glass at once. The bills will be sent to Los Angeles to be checked over, then you will receive your check in settlement from this office." He then wrote to W. H. Allen, informing him of the arrangement. "It is to be delivered on cars at Los Angeles. They guarantee against all breakage. Tell Elliott to hire a watchman for the new residence nights as soon as the carpenters commence work or as soon as there is anything around the building that will need watching and tell him to write how he is getting along."

On May 11th, T.D. addressed a letter to Elliott:

I have written to Andrea at Milwaukee today that he can put in the electric fittings in the residence at the price you name $425.00.

The greenhouse at the rear of the Stimson estate, ca. 1895. LAPL

I told him to commence the work at once. Have you ordered the screen doors and windows for the house. If not do so at once.

Also during that month, he made arrangements for Carsley Manufacturing to deliver to James H. Rice Co. all the art glass sash and the specifications for the vestibule doors. While in Chicago that month, T.D. made another purchase to ship west. He wrote his son Willard in Los Angeles on May 23:

I have bought a pair of carriage horses and also two saddle horses making four in all which I will ship to Los Angeles on Wednesday of this week. It will take about seven days for them to go through. I have hired a man to go through with them who will also work for me as coachman when he arrives. His name is Warren Myers and I think he is a good man…You can put the horses in the house barn and find a place for the man to stay. Have a couple of the teams at the depot with wagons to haul up the stuff.

On June 8, the furniture was on its way. Devendorf wrote:

I have finished loading your car today and enclose the bill of lading of same A.T. and S.F. Car 6401 freight $225.00 prepaid. The buggies went in all right. I have loaded everything and if we had more stuff could of got it in as there's some spare room. I had J. A. Colby and Sons put in the cabinet that Mrs. Stimson bought of them and which she said to put in the car with Carsley's because I had plenty of room and thought it best to load it. The mirrors in this cabinet were not in same but will be shipped in a few days by Colby at their expense by express. The furniture from Tobey's is all in. Two boxes of clocks from Spauldings. One box of books from McClurg. One box of pictures from Thurper. Two boxes of books

Hotel Monte Vista in Monterey, California, a popular winter vacation destination for T.D. Stimson during the 1890s. SMC

The Figueroa Street residence, 1989.
Lawrence Kreisman (LK)

Romanesque columned entrance
porch. LK

and one box of pictures from the house. Three wagons from Birdsell. And I bought a piano from Chickering and put that in. It cost $500.00 which I paid and enclose the Bill with a 5 year Warrent. It is mahogany, upright, and is the finest that Chickering makes for a residence. It includes a stool and cover which I placed under one of the wagons. I think it is a trifle darker than you may like but Chickering is making all mahogony cases dark and I could not get a light one.

Other shipments followed as they were ready. On June 10, Devendorf wrote, "The Broswick and Balke folks say your billiard table will be ready today but I will not do anything about it until Carsley gets a car ready that we can put it in." On June 18th, he "was down at Orr and Locketts this morning and they will ship today all the hardware except that for the second floor which they haven't received from the manufacturer. They have written a letter and will hurry them up. I telephoned Carsley and he says

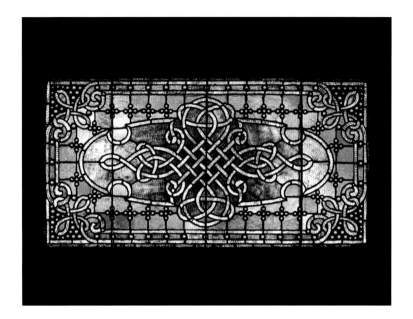

your sidetable for the dining room is all done and I suppose you will have to take it."

Other letters followed regarding furniture from the Wakefield Rattan Company and measurements for ceilings for the gas fixtures and the chandelier for the second floor hall. Stimson oversaw all of this inflow of materials and was interested always in finding the best stuff on the market. On July 28, Frank Devendorf wrote,

> Your telegram is at hand asking to ascertain which was the most durable mirror, the Mercury or Patent back. I went to see Sprague, Smith, and Co., George F. Kimball, and James H. Rice Co. and they all say that the Patent back is about the only kind of Mirror used now days. They don't keep the Mercury mirrors and say there are very few of them made. The Mercury back is more easily effected by the changes of weather which cause the spots in it. Also easily scratched.

The relationship between Carlsley Manufacturing and Stimson became strained mid-way through the process due to a misunderstanding about the extent of work Stimson expected and the amount F. M. Carlsley had provided according to their contract. During September and October, 1892, a heated correspondence developed. Carlsley had only been paid $20,000 for interior work, furniture, and upholstery amounting to $26,445.

The detail drawings furnished in most cases showed much more elaborate work than had been shown on the blueprints from which the firm had made its estimates. Carlsley had completed

Above left, Stained glass window in stair hall. LK

Above, Two of four art nouveau lancet windows illuminate the second and third floor landings. LK

Below, Neoclassical palmette carved pilaster in second floor bedroom. LK

the work as directed in the specifications, expecting that the changes would be paid for with a fair price. Some of the changes were outlined in an October 11th letter.

The brass thresholds we have nothing to do with, as we had wood ones there which we were not allowed to put down. The plaster mouldings are certainly extra as they were not shown at all on the original drawings at all and so with many other parts of the work which the detail drawings were very much elaborated. The doors had 5 or 6 more panels than original blue prints, nearly all the door and window casings were required to be 7/8 " thicker. The main stairs at the foot had two elaborate newel posts instead of one; also the hand rails had ramps and turnouts not in blue prints and many other things we will not mention here—there were ordered panelled jambs for 2d and 3d floors which also were not called for.

Heavily carved newell post of the principal staircase. LK

Threats, lawsuits, and lawyer's fees shadowed the firm and Stimson for nearly a year until a settlement could be reached. In the meantime, with all the furniture and fittings in Los Angeles, T.D. and Achsah could finally be "at home" and open their castle, with its transported interiors, to Los Angeles society.

Visitors to his estate eagerly passed along the palm tree-lined street through the formally planted lawns and up the steps to a marble colonnaded veranda and main entrance. They entered a panelled foyer—large enough to hold a grand piano and a substantial number of visitors—and were ushered into the front parlor or reception room, its sycamore walls and delicately ornamented plaster ceiling recalling a room in an English Tudor country home. Beyond was the principal parlor, framed by two carved Corinthian pillars and featuring a handsome marble fireplace and cupboards faced with bronze filigree grilles. Beyond the parlor was the formal dining room, with built-in corner china cabinet. Off to the right was Mr. Stimson's panelled study. A door led from here directly out to the veranda that wrapped around the north and east sides of the house. Between the dining room and the den was a hallway leading into the kitchen and pantry areas and the servant's stairs and halls. Below, the basement's arched doorways led to wine storage areas and a labyrinth of other rooms. A pipe organ had been part of the house as well, and its pipes were located in the basement.

The main stairway, with its heavily carved newel post, ascended past three stained glass windows to the second floor, where most of the bedrooms were located. Again, lavish use was made of hardwood wainscoting and trim mouldings in the classic style in both bedrooms and dressing/sitting rooms. Marble wash basins were enclosed behind wood-panelled cabinet doors. Between the second and third floor, four Art Nouveau lancet windows illuminated the stairway. The top floor was finished much more simply and had additional bedrooms used by the grandchildren, as well as substantial servants' quarters.

A small stairway led up to the turret of the home's tower. From here, the family could see in all directions for many miles. And it was from here that Stimson probably retreated at times to look north at the prominent silhouette of his most visible achievement, The Stimson Block, the centerpiece in what was fast becoming the commercial heart of Los Angeles.

THE PUBLIC REALM

Stimson wrote from Los Angeles to a Chicago friend, H. H. Getty on June 11, 1891:

> My property here is doing nicely and the rents are paid very promptly and nearly all occupied. I feel very well satisfied with my investments here and my change in business.[6]

He had much of which to be proud. Over twenty year's time, he had amassed a great deal of valuable timber acreage in the Midwest and Pacific Northwest, established successful saw and shingle mills in Michigan and Seattle, and operated a sales office in Chicago. While in the midst of construction on the Los Angeles house, Stimson began to liquidate his Midwest holdings to support the purchase of downtown Los Angeles properties and to develop them into office and hotel blocks.

During his Los Angeles years, his reputation rapidly shifted from that of lumberman to that of banker, developer, and capitalist. He was director of various financial institutions, including the Citizens' Bank (of which he owned the majority of stock), and for a time a vice president of the Chamber of Commerce. His interests ranged from real estate to railroading to tourist services. He was, for example, instrumental in the gifting of Griffith Park to the city in

---

6. Stimson Mill Company Records.

Above, Stimson Block at Third and Spring Streets, ca. 1920. LAPL

1896. But the Stimson Block at Third and Spring Streets put the city on notice that he was a powerful force in the shaping of Los Angeles.

According to a letter from W. H. Allen to Stimson on May 20, 1892, Willard was left in charge of interviewing potential architects for the project. "Willard has been overrun with architects for several days, but has finally selected Brown's plans. He has not got his figures yet. I took a look at the inside finish at the residence yesterday. It is *very* fine."

The Stimson Block architecture reflected the then-popular Romanesque Revival style and was, according to a contemporary tabloid, *Contractor*, "one of the largest and finest business buildings in the city." It was a six-story office building faced with Roman brick, terra cotta, carved stone, and wrought iron. It was typical of buildings with which Stimson would have been familiar in Chicago, including Daniel Burnham's 1883 Rookery, in which he had invested. In its corner siting, the rounded corner turret and four-story window bays that embellished both street facades, and its rich variety of semi-round arched windows and terra cotta decorative panels, the building also closely recalled architect Elmer Fisher's Pioneer and Burke Buildings constructed in Seattle after the1889 fire. They too would have been familiar to Stimson from his visits there to inspect the family lumber holdings his sons C.D. and Frederick were then managing.[7]

Carroll Brown's designs for the facades were flamboyant. He had included a group of four open, Roman-arched balcony surrounds with pierced stone balconets—similar to the one at Stimson's Figueroa Street residence. The spandrels between floors were decorated with bands of terra cotta ornament that progressed upward to a very rich tapestry of blind panels, acanthus borders, and leaf and vine ornament at the parapet. The structural brick piers visibly lightened as they rose two floors, then split into two, and finally, at the top floor, into three parts.

For the Stimson Block, T.D. was forging new territory. He knew little about what was involved in developing a commercial property from the ground up. He sent plans to Devendorf that called for steel I beams carried on steel I-bar columns "which will have to be covered with terra cotta as a protection against fire." The facades were to be built "of terra cotta and brick of the Roman pattern." Devendorf researched skyscrapers being built in Chicago and provided him with information, costs, and delivery dates for iron and steel, fittings, and boiler systems. He went to some of the new buildings to see what

Top, The Rookery, designed by Burnham and Root. J. M. Taylor. CCL

Below, The Pioneer Building, designed by Elmer Fisher. UW

7. Ironically, for a short period in the 1890s, Brown was a partner with Elmer Fisher, the star of Northwest Romanesque architecture, whose Pioneer Building design of 1889 was promoted as widely as Brown's Stimson Block. Fisher had relocated to Los Angeles in 1893 and his fortunes and opportunities dwindled. Ultimately, he gave up his office in the Stimson block and ended his years in obscurity as a carpenter. In a letter dated June 13, 1896, he sells his desk, cabinets, screens, chairs, rugs to Stimson for one dollar. Stimson Mill Company Records.

kind of engine and boiler they used to hoist brick and mortar, and received estimates from major steel companies in the Chicago area and as far east as Pittsburgh.

Into September, Devendorf received estimates from several steel companies, but no one was able to deliver the columns on Stimson's timetable, which required iron for the first floor delivered by the 25th of October. Devendorf favored Illinois Steel, but that firm would not agree to make the first delivery before December 15. They also "make some criticisms of your architect's specifications...some of the iron is much heavier than they think is required for such a building." He sought additional estimates, and the South Halsted Street Ironworks came in very favorably. In addition, they agreed "to pay all freight, cartage, and set the steel up complete in the building, even offering to give it the second coat of paint for $30.00 per net ton. They think they could have the material on the ground and start on the first floor by Nov. 15th."

Stimson eventually opted for local suppliers for structural ironwork. He chose James G. Fair's San Francisco company, Pacific Rolling Mill. The final carload was delivered by April, 1893, behind schedule "on account of the many additions made by your architect and which you had encorporated in the new contract." Stimson considered a Los Angeles firm to provide sills, sash columns, iron stairs, ornamental iron railing, and lights for the new building. Finally, he chose the Winslow Brothers Architectural Iron Works in Chicago for the job. He also went to Chicago's George Kimball for plate glass. But he went just down the block at 225 South Broadway to the Los Angeles Furniture Company for window shades.

While the iron supplier was being decided upon, Devendorf was also searching for the best prices on hardwoods—white oak, red oak, red birch, and birdseye maple. He recommended some quarter-sawn sycamore as an alternative—"it is beautiful and only is about $35.00 per M (as opposed to maple $150 per M)." During 1892-93, orders were made to the T. Wilce Co. of Chicago and the J. A. Holmes Co. of St. Louis for red oak. In May of that year, the Baker Iron Works was paid $4650 to arrange for the purchase, finish, and installation of two Otis hydraulic high speed passenger elevators. Various delays in their delivery were frustrating to Stimson. But this was typical. On September 20, 1892, Stimson wrote a curt note to Union Pressed Brick and Terra Cotta Co. in Vallejo, California, "When will you ship balance my Terra Cotta?" On October 5, Devendorf wrote to Merchant and Co. of Philadelphia to complain about improperly made tile,

Your letter to Mr. C.H. Brown of 27th has been handed to me
in regard to the tile which you shipped him on August 24th as per

T.D. Stimson, ca. 1895. DSB

your invoice of that date amounting to $170.00 These tiles will not fit the tower roof and will have to be made to fit which is not only costly but is a great inconvenience.

On November 8, five boxes of copper tile were shipped back to the manufacturer. These unexpected mixups forced them to delay the work of stone masons from the Chatain Galetti Ornamental Stone Co. of San Francisco. That and other unexpected costs and changes accounted for Stimson's November 4 request to borrow $20,000 for 4 months at 6% interest from the Merchant's National Bank. "I need this amount to complete my building." By the time of completion, the project had cost in excess of $800,000.

The shortage of proper materials, misunderstandings with suppliers, and incorrect specifications that occurred with both the house and office block construction—even though C.H. Brown was not responsible for much of it—cooled Stimson's relationship with him. Asked to write a letter of recommendation for his architect, on April 13 he wrote a short and non-committal note, "Mr. C. H. Brown was the Architect of my Residence and Stimson Block and has proven very satisfactory to me. The buildings will speak for themselves." Stimson would look elsewhere for architects on his next few projects.

The experience had also sapped his strength. As he coped with various illnesses during 1892-94, he made provision for dispensing of his properties and investments. He made some initial moves in that direction in 1892 when, as Christmas presents, he gifted the Seattle properties to C.D., Ezra, and Fred. Willard received the ranch Stimson had purchased in 1891 from Detroit owner Simon Murphy eight miles east of Los Angeles. It was valued at $20,000, with horses and stock an additional $5,000. Ezra received a house T.D. had bought "a short time ago, for $10,000," and lots valued at $6,500. Mrs. Stimson was given the residence. In 1894, Fay received property in Atkinson, Nebraska; mill property at Muskegon; the Big Rapids property; and "any and all the lands I own in the State of Michigan except the housing property in Ingraham County which I reserve for my sister." Mrs. Stimson was given the Stimson Block and shares in Columbia Savings. "I had intended this as next Christmas presents but owing to my illness have concluded to give it now. If nothing happens I hope we will all be together here next Christmas though the presents are given in advance." He recovered fully and continued to follow his interest in city development.

While other substantial four-and five-story office blocks surrounded it, Stimson's six-story building was, for a short while, considered the city's first skyscraper. In 1888, Major George

Bonebrake and his business associate John Bryson erected a five-story building at the corner of Spring and Second Streets. In 1891, the Bradbury estate erected its five-story Bradbury block, noted for its wrought iron lightcourt, on the southeast corner of Broadway and Third. The Stimson Block would not be topped until 1897, when Colonel J. B. Lankershim built the seven-story Lankershim Building directly across the street. Christian Henne, one of the city's early brewers built his L-shaped Henne Building a year later by enclosing the Lankershim Building on two sides. Not to be outdone by Lankershim, T.D. Stimson started planning an eight-story building to be known as the Douglas Block for property he owned on the northwest corner of Third and Spring.[8]

While Stimson's enterprises were not completely insulated from the nationwide depression of those years, his decision to cash out his midwest land and real estate holdings was made at a fortunate time, and he was able to place his fortune into downtown Los Angeles. He saw there much potential for growth because of the admirable climate, Pacific trade routes, and greater west coast timber resources than existed in the nearly completely depleted midwest forests. And Los Angeles, feeling much of the inertia of the rest of the county, was a bargain hunter's delight in its land prices.

Shortly after the Stimson Block was completed, and during the period when the ideas for some of his smaller, income-producing buildings were being developed, the name of Stimson was suggested in architectural and building industry circles as a potential source for future commissions.

As early as 1893, with economic recovery quite a distance in the future, Stimson bought, maintained, or built buildings in and around Broadway and South Third Street. Contractors who had worked on his first building along with newcomers in the building trades, applied to be considered on his next projects. Referrals and support letters from important business associates paved the way for solicitations from several highly respected architectural firms in Los Angeles, San Francisco, Minneapolis, and Chicago.[9]

San Franciscan and California State Senator James G. Fair, President of Pacific Rolling Mill Company, had supplied the steelwork for the Stimson Block. On June 12, 1893, he recommended his own architect, Henry A. Schulze, who wrote to Stimson that same day:

---

8. The Stimson Block was remodelled by architect Robert H. Orr for King Investment Company according to a note in *Builder and Contractor* (Dec.1939): 32, 1. The entire building was demolished in 1963 to become a parking lot.

9. The following excerpts are drawn from letters in the Stimson Mill Company Records.

I have been informed that you are about to commence extensive improvements to your properties in Los Angeles and would most respectfully solicit your clientage if you have not already employed an architect. I refer with permission to the Hon. James G. Fair of this city whose architect I have been for the past six years during which time I have built many large buildings for him. I was the architect for the Mark Hopkins Estate here and am now doing work for Mr. Timothy Hopkins. I built the very costly residence of Mr. Henry J. Crocker just completed in this city and have built and am now building for his cousin Mr. Chas. H. Crocker. I was the architect of the new Club House of the Olympic Club just completed and am now building an extensive office building at Bakersfield for Mr. Lloyd Tevis. I would also refer to Mr. Maurice Casey of the McLaughlin Estate for whom I have built large and extensive improvements. I could mention many other well known men by whom I have been regularly employed through a number of years and to whom I could refer you for my credentials.

Trusting that, should you contemplate employing an architect, I may receive your favorable consideration, I am, Most Respectfully Yours,

Henry A. Schulze

Engraving from letterhead, office of T.D. Stimson, ca. 1900. SMC

Word of Stimson's building efforts spread to the depressed Midwest as well and drew inquiries from well-established architects when building starts in their own hometowns were few and far between. The firm of George E. Bertrand and Walter J. Keith wrote from their offices in the Lumber Exchange in Minneapolis on November 17, 1894, to offer their services.

Last winter when our Mr. Keith called on you in Los Angeles in regard to your proposed new building you were kind enough to invite him to call upon you again this winter as at that time you expected to be ready to decide upon your plans.

The Dayton Building here, in which you were interested and of which Mr. Keith left you a cut and which cost complete, ready for occupany, $123,000, has been highly successful, being absolutely fireproof, and is now returning a revenue of $30,000 a year, we are informed by the manager.

Will you kindly inform us about when you will be ready to take up the building matter and whether you contemplate the erection of more than one building the coming year. If there is going to be enough heavy building in your city, we want to establish ourselves at once, for in our judgement it is only a question of time when you will have a large commercial center there, and the climate is perfection.

Coming, as it was, during the first taste of a harsh Minnesota winter, these last remarks hint at the tantalizing qualities of Los Angeles as a business destination apart from the economic climate there.

Local architect Alfred Beck—who had formerly worked for H. Carroll Brown—wrote Stimson from the firm of Morgan Wells in Los Angeles in early 1895:

> You know full well that your present building was designed and detailed (as far as brickwork, wood and terra cotta is concerned) by myself. I am with Morgan and Wells permanently and of course would like to get your work into this office.

In March, Stimson made the decision to build on his property on the northeast corner of Broadway and Third. He demolished the existing buildings at 312—Third and 307-9 South Broadway and hired local architect A.M. Edelman. On May 21,1895, Edelman sent Stimson the plans and specifications for two buildings—one two-story and the adjacent three-story on Third between Broadway and Hill Street that comprised a rooming house with 42 rooms called the Spencer Block.

While still in construction, Stimson already contemplated a flagship building for the northwest corner of Third and Spring Street across from the Stimson Block. It would be called The Douglas Building and, at eight stories tall, would tower over its companion. While overseeing rents and tenant leases, keeping track of his timber and mill investments, and raising funds for the new building, Stimson also surveyed the field of accomplished architects for one who would suit his project.

One of the architects Stimson passed over in his decision-making was the designer of the Auditorium Building in which Stimson had invested so heavily—-Louis Sullivan. He actively solicited work outside of the Midwest after the dissolution of his partnership with Dankmar Adler, relying upon business associates he had made in Chicago to introduce him to real estate developers who were planning projects.

Engraving of Douglas Building, as built.

DOUGLAS BUILDING

On August 13, 1896, Martin A. Ryerson, son of the million-aire Chicago businessman who had been Stimson's friend and business associate, wrote a praise-filled letter of introduction for Sullivan. For that family, Sullivan had designed the Jewelers' Building (1881-82), Alexander H. Revell Furniture Company (1881-83), Martin A. Ryerson Building(1884), the Ryerson Charities Trust Building(1886), a tomb for the father at Graceland Cemetary (1887), and another Ryerson Building (1887) redesigned and built as the Walker Warehouse (1888-90). Ryerson's letter was accompanied by a handwritten letter from Louis Sullivan dated August 17, 1896:

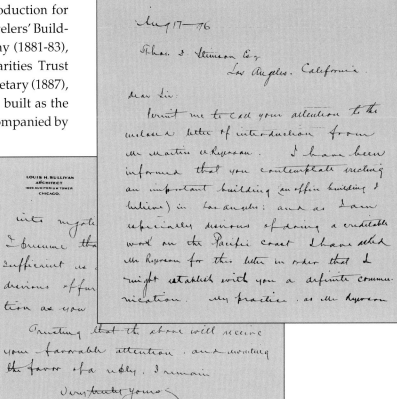

Dear Sir:

Permit me to call your attention to the enclosed letter of introduction from Mr. Martin Ryerson. I have been informed that you contemplate erecting an important building (an office building I believe) in Los Angeles: and as I am especially desirous of doing a creditable work on the Pacific Coast I have asked Mr. Ryerson for this letter in order that I might establish with you a definite communication. My practice as Mr. Ryerson suggests has been large. It has also been quite varied covering almost every class of building both as to use and as to cost. I have found distance to be no impediment to the success of my undertakings: having satisfactorily erected buildings in New York, Buffalo, New Orleans, St. Louis, Pueblo, Colorado, Salt Lake City. I therefore feel not the slightest doubt that I could give you thoroughly satisfactory service and give you the benefit of Chicago methods, which have become highly developed during the last ten years. If it is in fact your intention to build, it will give me great pleasure to offer you my services as architect, and to enter into negotiations to that end. I presume that what I have written is sufficient as a preliminary, but I am desirous of furnishing you as full information as you may desire.

Trusting that the above will receive your favorable attention, and awaiting the favor of a reply, I remain

Very truly yours,

Louis H. Sullivan

Sullivan's efforts to find work on the Pacific Coast date back to 1890. Probably on the basis of their Auditorium Building and Pueblo, Colorado Opera House, Adler and Sullivan were chosen to design an opera house for Seattle, Washington. Preliminary plans

and elevations were made in 1890 and Charles Bebb, as superin-
tending architect, journeyed to Seattle. (Coincidentally, it was
Charles Bebb who supervised construction of C.D. Stimson's Mi-
nor Avenue house from 1899-1901 and was the architect for the
Frederick Stimson house in 1903). Financing difficulties halted the
project in construction and it never proceeded.[10] Unfortunately,
Sullivan's effort to get work in Los Angeles was a dead-end too.
Frank Devendorf, having closed down the Chicago South Water
Street office in early 1893, had moved to Los Angeles to assist
Stimson there. He had written to Sullivan, informing him that
Stimson was out of town. In a follow-up letter, dated November 17,
1896, Sullivan wrote:

> Referring to my letter of Aug. 17th accompanied by a letter
> of introduction from Mr. Martin A. Ryerson. In your absence from
> the city my letter was answered by your Mr. Devendorf who stated
> that owing to the unsettled conditions you would not build during
> the year.
>
> May I now enquire if the election of McKinley is causing you
> to again take up the idea of building the structure to which I
> referred, and if I may be of service to you in that connection.
>
> Awaiting the esteemed favor of your reply I am
>
> Very truly yours,
>
> Louis H. Sullivan

It would not have helped Sullivan's case to mention
McKinley favorably since T.D. was a life-long Democrat. There
appear to be no letterpress copies to indicate that Sullivan's last
letter received a response. However, it would have only reconfirmed
that Stimson's office block was still on hold. Sullivan's queries,
along with a ponderous amount of other correspondence, was set
aside and possibly forgotten by the time T.D. Stimson finally
committed resources to the Douglas Building project.

By December of 1897, T.D. had decided to give the well-
respected firm of James and Merritt Reid of San Francisco the
design contract for the building. He had made business trips to San
Francisco and vacationed at the Hotel del Coronado near San
Diego; in both places, he would have heard of their reputation and
could have admired their built designs.

James and Merritt Reid were considered among the leading architects of commercial buildings on the West Coast at the

---

10. Jeffrey Karl Ochsner and Dennis Alan Andersen, "Adler and Sullivan's
Seattle Opera House Project," *Journal of the Society of Architectural Historians*
XLVIII(Sept. 1989):223-231.

time. James had been educated at McGill University in Montreal and had gone on to architectural training at Massachusetts Institute of Technology and at the Ecole des Beaux Arts in Paris. As such, he would have been one of the earliest Americans to study there, along with Richard Morris Hunt and Charles McKim. While working as a draftsman in Indiana in 1888, James Reid was offered the opportunity to design a new resort hotel at Coronado near San Diego. Afterward, he joined Merritt in his brother's San Francisco practice and together they designed many commercial and residential buildings prior to and after the earthquake and fire and until retirement in 1932. Commissions brought them to southern California as well. Stimson's project—and the offer of office space in the Stimson Block—would have appealed to the firm as they saw that city slowly digging out from under the lethargy of the beginning of the decade.[11]

The architects established a temporary office in the Stimson Block and set to work. On December 15, 1897 their progress report indicated they had figured the loads down to the level of the second floor, the shapes were determined to some point, and the plans

11. The Fitzhugh Building and the Merritt Office Building at Eighth and Broadway in Los Angeles were later designs. Withey, *Biographical Dictionary*, 50; *Who's Who in California 1928-29*, 313; *California Arts and Architecture* (Feb. 1929): 68.

Hotel del Coronado, designed by James Reid, ca. 1890. SMC

Spring and Third Streets, ca. 1920.
Douglas Building (left) and
Stimson Building (right). LAPL

Decorative terra cotta grille above
ground floor facade LK

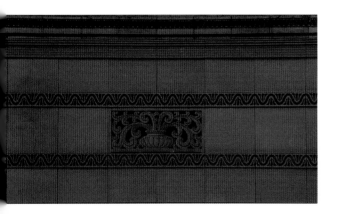

were "pretty well worked up on small scale and now being developed in detail."

The plans called for 46 rooms on each floor. The interior was to be lighted by a court approximately 36 x 62 feet from the second floor to the roof covered by a skylight at the second floor. An 8 foot corridor would extend around the entire building, opening to the rooms on either side. Two elevators would be finished in marble and tile. The stairways were to be of iron and marble with iron grille enclosures for the elevators.

While the plans were being finalized, on January 31, 1898, T.D. Stimson died at his Figueroa Street house. The Douglas Building, in an abbreviated five-story form, was completed in 1900 as a memorial to the lumber baron turned real estate mogul.

An early notice of the intent of the Stimson heirs to follow through on their father's wishes was published in *Builder and Contractor* on April 6, 1898.

Architect Reid Brothers, 401-402 Stimson Block have the

plans and specifications of the New Douglas Build-ing for the Stimson estate all ready for bidders. The work will be let separate or as a whole. April 14 is the date set for the letting of the work. The building will be five stories and basement; the el-evation will be either stone or pressed brick and terra cotta; steel columns and girders throughout; wood floor joists forming a semi-fire proof struc-ture. Inside finish may possibly be oak.

The Douglas Block was remarkably sub-dued—even severe—in comparison to Stimson's earlier venture. The facades of smooth tan face brick were punctuated by single windows equally spaced. The corner was curved—a distinctly modern recollection of the ornate corner bays of earlier buildings like the Stimson Block. Horizontal brick banding visually separated the retail floor from the offices above. The banding also related to additional mouldings below and above the top-floor window and along the over-hanging cornice with its dentil moulding. Applied decorative ornament was scarce. There were stone sur-rounds for the second floor windows, each with festooned shield crowns and dentil-moulded cornices.

Despite its seeming severity and the reworking of the design that lowered its planned height, the building was considered among Los Angeles' greatest office buildings and commanded the highest rentals. In its early years, it housed the chief ticket office of the Southern Pacific Railroad. Its reputation might have had much to do with the prestige of its architects.

T.D. Stimson died of heart failure on the morning of Monday, January 31, 1898. By five o'clock The *Evening Express* carried the story on its front page.

The dignified facade has a gently curving corner and warm hued Roman brick. LK

Egg and dart, leaf, and dentil moulding embellish the crown cornice. LK

Although he was one of the wealthiest men in this section of the State, Mr. Stimson was simple in his tastes and manners, and always approachable by those who had business with him. He gave close and critical attention to the details of all matters in which he took an interest. While his Third-street block was in process of erection, no day laborer on the structure worked harder than he did. He was emphatically a self-made man, and that fact showed in all his business transactions, and also in his point of view of the world's affairs.

Of all the accolades, perhaps the most generous appeared in the February 5 issue of *Greater Los Angeles*, a weekly tabloid "devoted to the interests of Southern California."

He came here during blue times, and commenced launching out until he had spent a cool million of dollars in city lots and improvements of the most imposing and substantial kind. He it was who built so liberally and so handsomely on Spring Street as to create a permanent business heart to our city and which enhanced many-fold all realty between First and Second streets on Spring and Broadway and held up Main from decay and on all the cross streets between those named above. Every man and woman who owned property in any of these thoroughfares were made richer by the citizenship of T.D. Stimson. He also gave Figueroa street an enhancement that has made it a boulevard that will in time be the prettiest in the world by erecting a $150,000 residence that will long remain a monument in his honor...It was by reason of his coming here with his family and rearing pretentious structures that brought other Chicago men of means to this section.

Stimson was viewed by Los Angelenos with respect for his fair dealings and appreciation for having invested so substantially in the growing city, both in terms of its real estate and in good works. Obituaries and editorials shortly after his death expressed similar sentiments to that of the Rev. Bert Estes Howard at the funeral service on Thursday, February 3, 1898 in the Stimson residence.

In days to come, when one shall inquire for the monument of Thomas Douglas Stimson, men may point to our busy streets and to our city filled with the hum of traffic and industry and say: "This is his monument."

The estate was settled some time after his death. Partly this was due to a stipulation in his will that the partition should be made when the youngest grand-child—Harold Stimson of Seattle—reached his majority. Consequently, on October 9, 1913, the *Los Angeles Times* reported "Split Millions Among Dozen. Great Stimson Estate Divided Out of Court." The $2.5 million estate was divided equally among twelve heirs—four children and eight grand-children. Each received $208,335. Benefactors were Willard H. Stimson and his son, Charles (Cully); Ezra T. Stimson; Charles D. Stimson and his children, Thomas D. and Dorothy; Fred Stimson and his children; Mrs. Walter Leeds and Louis D. and Clarence S., children of the late Mrs. Olive J. Fay, daughter of Thomas D.

The real estate holdings had been substantial. Willard and his son "Cully" retained ownership of the Douglas Block at Third and Spring, completed in 1900. Charles D. and Frederick S. and their children received the Muskegon building at Third Street and Broadway (a site that would be the future home of the magnificent Million Dollar Theatre), and the Allen Flats on Seventh and Spring Street. Ezra Stimson received cash and mortgages, including the family house. Louis D. and Clarence S. Fay received downtown property consisting of 110 feet on Spring Street between Third and Fourth Streets and 60 feet on Spring Street between Second and Third Streets.

Achsah Jane Stimson lived on in the Figueroa Street home with Ezra until her death in 1904. She actively managed the leasing of the downtown properties and made daily decisions about tenants, maintenance, and repairs. She continued to contribute to the causes of education and social welfare. An abcess of the liver, a chronic condition from which she had suffered for two years, confined her to bed for the final four months of her life. This must have been greatly disturbing to her because she was not accustomed to a sedentary life. Not a few eyebrows must have been raised in Los Angeles social circles when in 1899, at the age of 65, she undertook to travel around the world on her own. Her travelling companion kept a sketchbook to recall visits to Japan, India, Turkey, and western Europe.

Achsah Stimson, ca. 1895. SMC

Above, Ezra Stimson residence on West Adams Street, 1989. LK

Below, House and garden of Ezra and Anne Stimson, ca. 1905. SMC

Her contributions were noted in a local obituary notice.

Mrs. Stimson was the founder of the Stimson-Lafayette Industrial School and made it a successful institution. No person, not even the members of her own family, knew the extent of her charities and hundreds of poor people were made happy through her generosity and kindness, but the world never knew what gifts she made. Being possessed of an independent fortune she devoted thousands of dollars every year to the relief of distress wherever she found it. Poor children were here special wards, and there are in the public schools of Los Angeles scores of children who were assisted in many ways by Mrs. Stimson. She was a member of the Ebell Club and until her last illness took an active interest in its affairs.

She and her husband set a memorable example for their children of how a family of means should behave in the broader world of politics, urban development, and social and moral purpose.

Ezra and his wife, Anne, continued to live in the family home on Figueroa Street after his father's death. When his mother died in 1904, he put the house up for sale[12] and hired Frederick Louis Roehrig (1857-1907), a prominent residential designer best known for the Green Hotel in Pasadena, to build a stately English-styled home on a site only two blocks away on West Adams Street. The multigabled granite and half-timber home, with its port-cochere, entrance porches, and broad overhanging roofs, would have been a popular and familiar type throughout America at that time. But its choice might have been stimulated by Ezra's visits to the Northwest. Both his brothers, C.D. in 1900 and Frederick in 1903, had completed impressive English-styled homes in Seattle. He may not have wished to be outdone by his siblings. Apart from its architecture, the home's most charming quality was its formally landscaped garden and fountain.

---

12. The house was sold to beer baron Edward Maier. In the 1940s, it was occupied by a University of Southern California fraternity. Rumor has it that a few too-noisy parties raised the ire of neighbor Estelle Doheny, who bought the house. She donated her own home and other properties on Chester Place to the Sisters of St. Joseph and retired to the Stimson House for some years. On her death, the Stimson property was also donated to what had become Mount St. Mary's College. Until recently, the house had been occupied as a residence hall. It is now vacant.

In Part IV of the *Los Angeles Sunday Times* of November 5, 1905, the Adams Street house was the featured photograph. The caption read, "Among the many beautiful and stately homes that adorn the fashionable West End is the imposing residence of E.T. Stimson, located at 825 West Adams Street—a residence that is pointed out to visitors as one of the most substantial abodes of elegance and good taste in Los Angeles."

After the death of T.D., W.H. carried on the family business in Los Angeles. He had moved to southern California not by choice but because of his health. In 1892, only two years after moving into a new home in Seattle, he traded his interest in the Stimson Mill Company for additional stock in the Stimson Land Company, and he and his wife Kate moved to Figueroa Street. After completing his schooling at the Throop Institute (now California Institute of Technology), their son C.W. (Cully) returned to Seattle to live with C.D. and Harriet in their Minor Avenue house and learn the lumber business from his uncle. In 1902, the Ballard Lumber Company was incorporated. Its president was W.H. of Los Angeles, and Cully was treasurer and general manager.

Like his father, W.H. (Willard) contributed much of his time to his adopted city, Los Angeles, serving as police commissioner from 1900 to 1904. When the Figueroa Street house was sold in 1904, Willard and Kate initially moved to the elegant Alexandria Hotel, the city's most fashionable hotel at the time. While this location at the center of social life in the city appealed greatly to Kate, Willard desired the peace and openness of the southern California countryside. He found his dream north of Los Angeles in Eagle Rock near Glendale. Here, on two of the 28 tracts that had originally comprised the Verdugo family ranch, W.H. had a comfortable 7-bedroom 5-bathroom Craftsman home built and planted 800 lemon trees, 30 avocado trees, numerous other fruit trees, and an arboretum of many other varieties. He landscaped the canyon at the rear of the house with imported vegetation, pines, palms, and shrubs. For 40 years, the ranch was a prize possession of the family.[13]

Birdseye view of W.H. Stimson's lemon ranch, showing Craftsman house at end of circular drive. TBS

13. Ross, 44-45.

Minor Avenue residence and porte cochere, ca. 1910. DSB

Background, North elevation drawing, C.D. Stimson residence. EWSHS

THE CHARLES DOUGLAS STIMSONS OF FIRST HILL

The ruins of the Occidental Hotel after the Seattle Fire, June, 1889.
DSB

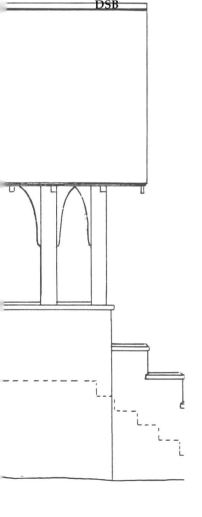

In 1898, Seattle's First Hill looked more like a clearcut than a home to Seattle's prominent families. During the preceding decades, the native growth fir of the hill, located a steep climb up from the bustling waterfront, had been completely leveled. This, if anything, probably had a positive effect upon First Hill's early development as a residential neighborhood.

The 1889 Seattle Fire that destroyed most of the commercial district had also cleared houses and churches in the pioneer city. In some ways, the fire was considered fortuitous. Commercial interests needed to expand. Parishioners and their church fathers took this opportunity to consider moving away to the relative safety and quiet respectability of the upper avenues and to First Hill and Queen Anne Hill.

THE PRIVATE REALM

The C.D. Stimsons and their son had lived at First North and Ward Street on lower Queen Anne Hill north of downtown since 1888. While not modest, it probably seemed crowded with the birth of a daughter Dorothy Frances, in 1892. By 1898, Stimson had done quite well with the mill business. He had been helped financially by the 1889 fire, the Yukon Gold Rush, the influx of many new families to the area, and the resulting platting and sale

of home lots throughout the city. The substantial homes of Seattle's
first families would not have escaped his eye, nor would he have
wanted anything less than he could afford for his wife and children.
He saw First Hill as a suitable site for the new family home.

Through business and social connections in Spokane,
Stimson may have seen and admired the Tudor revival home of A.
B. Campbell, completed there in 1898. He also may have inquired
about its architect and met with Kirtland Cutter, whom he hired to
do a residence in Seattle. The similarities were not
lost on the Campbell family; they were not at all
pleased when they discovered how closely
Stimson's home resembled theirs.

Kirtland Cutter's firm, established in
Spokane on the eve of the great Spokane Fire of
1889, grew to be one of the most prolific in the state,
with a client list that read like a Who's Who of
industry and commerce. Born in Cleveland in 1860,
he attended the Brooks Military Academy, studied
at the Art Students' League in New York, and
proceeded to Europe for further study and travel.
Arriving in Spokane Falls in 1885, he worked at his
uncle's bank. Although he is reputed to have done
some architectural work during this time, it was

the Spokane Fire that inspired him to form a partnership with John Poetz and generated a great deal of commercial and residential work for the firm. When Poetz retired, Karl Gunnar Malmgren (1862-1921) became Cutter's partner. Together until 1917, they were a highly successful team.[1]

Cutter was an eccentric. He was reputed to have a collection of wigs that he changed periodically to give the impression that his hair was growing or newly cut. Such concern for minute details may seem frivolous; to Cutter, it was an essential part of his art. He was a master of the eclectic; his genius lay in an ability to combine the rich ornamental vocabularies of the various Classical, Romanesque, Moorish, Gothic, and Renaissance styles into successful residential architecture that was both grand in scale and yet comfortable to live in. Indeed, he seemed as comfortable working on a rustic Swiss chalet or log cabin as he was in creating a million dollar mansion. According to his contemporaries, Cutter was what might be called "the idea man." He was far more interested in design concepts than in the mechanics. Much of his success was based upon his partnership of nearly thirty years with Malmgren and the various skilled draftspeople who transformed his thumbnail sketches into workable designs—among them Carl Nuese, Edwin Wager, and Andrew Willatzen.[2]

Logged of its native timber, First Hill awaits homeowners, ca. 1895. MOHAI

For C.D. Stimson (as he had for A.B. Campbell and other notable clients), Cutter chose an English half-timbered style that harkens back to medieval England. Cutter was probably influenced by the late nineteenth century English Arts and Crafts designers—most notably William Morris, Philip Webb, Baillie Scott, and Norman Shaw— in his use of hand-adzed timbers, sawn decorative bargeboards, and mock rafter ends.

Local architects during the preceding decade had continued the practice of designing commodious Stick style and Queen Anne Style Victorians of wood frame construction with ornate trim and generously scaled verandas, porches, and bay windows. In many cases, these were simply pattern- book houses implanted locally by skilled carpenters with inexpensive sawn timber at their disposal. Cutter's English design, while gaining considerable

1. *Kirtland Kelsey Cutter: The Collection*, (Spokane, WA: Eastern Washington State Historical Society, n. d.), 54; and Edward W. Nolan, *A Guide to the Cutter Collection* (Spokane, WA: Eastern Washington State Historical Society, 1984).

2. Ibid.

Kirtland Kelsey Cutter, ca. 1900

Letter dated September 18, 1899
from Cutter to Stimson. DSB

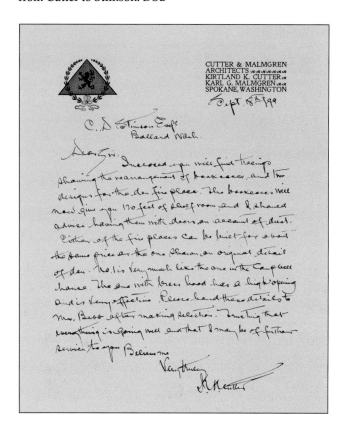

popularity elsewhere in the country by 1898, was just beginning to make its appearance on the West Coast. Local architects barely introduced it into their work, and certainly not on the scale that Cutter generated in the Stimson house. [3]

Kirtland Cutter wrote frequent letters to C.D. Stimson and his wife during the arduous two years of construction and interior decoration. These, along with inventory lists and invoices from 1899-1901, show that the architect was responsible for the complete decoration of the interior from wall colors, fabrics, and furniture down to the most minute finish details. The correspondence and interior photographs taken in 1901 reveal much about the practice of interior decoration early in the century. In particular, the letters explore the respectful relationship that evolved as Cutter educated his client to his vision of how the house should be furnished.[4]

In a letter to C. D. Stimson on May 9th, 1899, the architect assured his client, "This house we consider better in many respects than the Campbell house without being so expensive, though we are not at all certain, with the present interior detail work, that it will not exceed your limit of cost." As it turned out, the interior decoration and furnishings most certainly did exceed the initial limits of cost and at times also pushed the limits of the cordial relationship between Cutter and Mr. and Mrs. Stimson.

The 10,000-square-foot house had rooms of varied and specific character, spaces considered suitable for the daily activities of "men" or "women" at the turn of the century. Visitors entered the pointed arched doorway into the Romanesque entry hall. Columnettes with carved capitals supported a Roman barrel vault decorated with hand-painted red and gold canvas papers. Stairs led into the main hall and dining room. Furnishings originally included a chest, table, standing clock, armchair, footstool, and hall tree—all in Flemish or Gothic carved

3. Evidence of its coming vogue are seen in John Graham and David Myers' Elizabethan manor for the Hainsworth family in West Seattle in 1901. Charles Bebb, Cutter's superintendent of construction, built a substantial client list in homes of the style after completion of the Stimson property. Not coincidentally, one of these was Frederick Stimson, C.D.'s brother, for whom Bebb in partnership with Louis Mendel built a house on West Highland Drive in 1903-4.

4. Excerpts following are quoted from the Kirtland Cutter letters and inventory lists in the Dorothy Stimson Bullitt Archives.

oak. The doorways into the reception room, living room/library, and dining room were all fitted with red and gold Gothic tapestry draperies and pocket doors. Thirty rolls of Red Damask paper were used for the stair halls.

Of the decor, Cutter wrote, "The ceiling panels to be covered with gilded canvas which is to be decorated as per sketch, lacquered and toned down to an antique finish. The side walls and the walls over the arch leading to the stair hall and the soffet of this arch and the walls over the front door, to be covered in the same gilded canvas and decorated as per pencil sketch, in colors to harmonize with the ceiling decorations and all toned down to an antique finish, a shade deeper than the ceiling."

To the right of the entry, the main living room functioned as a library and a stage for evening musicales and plays performed by the children. It bore the characteristic dark oak and Gothic carvings of an English manor house and was dominated by a huge Gothic hearth supported with hand-carved lions and magnificent copper and steel dragon andirons—a room with the qualities of a private men's club. The walls were covered in green and yellow Gothic tapestry fabric. Furniture included a mahogany table, sofa, bench, and armchairs, a wicker chair, oak writing desk and chair, a teakwood taboret, and four large down pillows. The velvet draperies repeated the Gothic quatrefoil motifs in the woodwork and window mouldings throughout the house.

C.D. Stimson, ca. 1900. DSB

Living room, view toward "stage."
1901. DSB

Reception room with French Empire furnishings, 1901. DSB

Ceiling plasterwork, reception room. Greg Gilbert (GG)

By contrast, to the left of the entry was a light-colored, delicately plastered neoclassical parlor in the style of Percier and Fontaine with Empire fireplace and furniture where Mrs. Stimson could receive her friends and serve tea during the day when she was "at home" to callers. (In that circle, ladies would choose a specific afternoon to be home that would not conflict with any of the other ladies. Mrs. Stimson was "at home" on Thursdays to First Hill ladies). The walls were panelled in yellow Empire damask. Cutter specified embroidered green silk velour for furnishings and 46 yards of Wilton carpet and border. The room was filled with mahogany furniture with gold ormula mountings that matched the Empire styled mahogany mantel and mirror.[5]

Directly up the stairs and past the stair hall was an English Tudor dining room reminiscent of Woolsey's closet at Hampton Court, with rich sycamore panelling and scenes of medieval court life painted on corduroy above the wainscotting. A dramatic blue-glass tiled fireplace with carved leaf and vine mantel and handsome brass sconces was the focal point of the room. Appropriately enough, the frieze above it included a king and his court seated at a banquet table, about to enjoy the feast. Furniture included a Flemish Oak

5. In 1914, the Joshua Green family replaced the fabric panels with plaster friezes that further reinforced the room's neoclassical ceiling and coving. From then on, the Greens referred to the reception room as the Empire room.

Above, Dining room glass tile fireplace. Frieze shows king and court at table. GG

Below, English Renaissance styled dining room with glass tiled fireplace, 1901. DSB

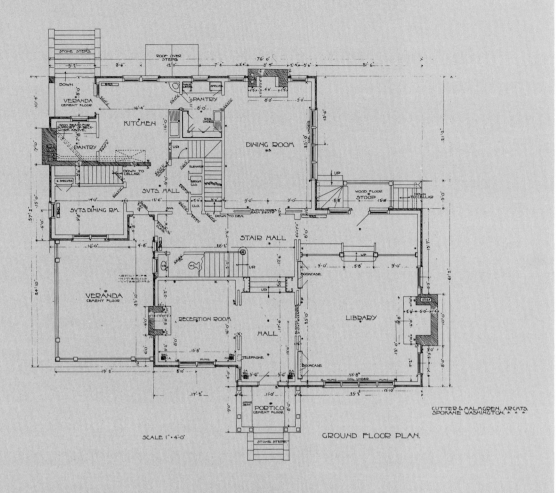

SCALE 1"=4'-0"   GROUND FLOOR PLAN.

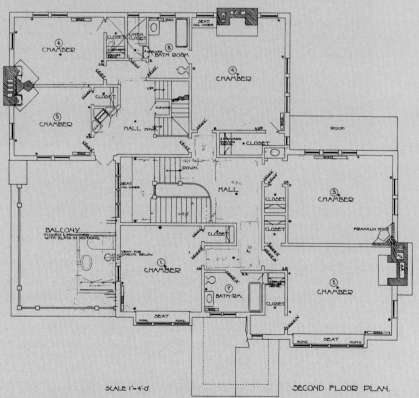

SCALE 1"=4'-0"   SECOND FLOOR PLAN.

Main and second floor plans, C.D.
Stimson residence. EWSHS

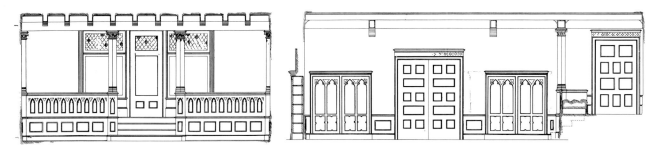

SCALE 1"=2'0"

Above, Library stage and gothic bookcase elevations. EWSHS

Below, West or front elevation. EWSHS

Right, North elevation. EWSHS

RESIDENCE FOR C.D. STIMSON. ESQ.
SEATTLE. WASHINGTON.

WEST ELEVATION.

CUTTER & MALMGREN.
ARCHITECTS.
SPOKANE. WASH.

SCALE 1"= 4'

**Turkish den and smoking room,
1901. DSB**

sideboard, serving table, china cabinet, and a dining table with twelve sidechairs and two armchairs. Drapes were of blue velour trimmed with tapestry border. A dark blue Indian rug was recommended of a size that would leave two feet of floor uncovered all round.

While the principal entertaining rooms were drawn from Western European traditions, the Middle East did not go unnoticed. The most exotic space in the house was the den adjoining the billiard room in the basement. It had been inspired by the prediliction during that era for Moorish smoking rooms where the men could retreat after dinner to play cards, drink brandy, and discuss the latest business deals. Its brass filigree Mosque lanterns, teakwood taboret, Oriental carpets, and the choice of saturated colors and patterns for fabrics and wall coverings captured the flavor of the "casbah." For this room, Cutter ordered Oriental silk window draperies, an ornately carved octagon poker table, and a couch with a middle eastern motif in a wool canvas fabric.

By contrast, the upstairs bedrooms were light-filled and bright with floral wallpapers and white painted moulding. Each had its own fireplace distinguished by a different color tile facing. The bathrooms had the latest in marble sinks and white enamel pedestal tubs with chrome fixtures. Extremely generous closets with built-in drawers to accommodate the extensive wardrobes of the family would have been a welcome change from earlier houses where huge armoires and chests of drawers were imperative.

Cutter's correspondence reveals a cordial, polite relationship developing between the client and the architect—a prerequisite for someone interested in building his practice with the wealthy. He was always attentive, and his constant—sometimes daily—correspondence kept the client abreast of any new ideas he or his draftspeople had for changes. He also kept Mr. Stimson apprised of the costs for items or services and suggested alternatives where appropriate. He saw to it that every facet of the job was completed to the satisfaction of the Stimsons and apologized when, for one reason or another, there were inconvenient delays or changes.

Two inventory lists were prepared. One was an estimate for furnishing the house, the other arrived with the furnishings and was checked off as each piece of furniture, lighting fixture, drapery, or decorative accessory entered the doors of the

Second floor bedroom, 1901. DSB

new home. Some lighting fixtures, brass hardware, locks, and wallpapers were selected from catalogues. Some, along with furnishings, were manufactured to Cutter's sketches and specifications or were ordered through W. L. Otis, a Cleveland, Ohio firm with which Cutter did much business. Cutter had grown up in Cleveland and had many contacts there, having had a branch office in Cleveland from 1895-1897. He also maintained that east coast worksmanship was superior. In his letter to Stimson of Dec. 16, 1899, he wrote, "We are enclosing scale detail of a combination gun case and side board for your den, on which we are getting an estimate from an Eastern Manufacturer of Furniture as the work would be much more satisfactory if made in this way, than by a local mill, as the mills have not the facilities for doing fine Cabinet work."

On Dec. 18 of that year he wrote:

We are just in receipt of bids from three first class carvers on the large Gothic lions for your Library fireplace, the lowest being $275.00. This seems a rather *stiff* price, but as the work is very difficult and can only be properly executed by an artist, we do not consider it unreasonable. There certainly are no wood carvers on this coast who can do justice to this class of work, the reason being that there is not enough of it done to keep a high priced sculptor constantly employed.

On January 29,1900, claiming to have spent several weeks "looking up the best and most artistic things to be found in this country," Cutter prepared estimates for decorations, furnishings, and fixtures and shipped the Stimsons a box containing sketches, photographs and fabrics,"..showing designs, materials and colorings as in my judgment they should be used to produce the most satisfactory results. The scheme for treatment throughout is to me altogether the most satisfactory which I have planned." He eased his client's worries about costs by mentioning that "while the estimate runs higher, perhaps, than you expected, I know from both past and present experience that the same things which we have specified would cost you in New York or Chicago 25% more than our figures."

In justifying the expense of some of the furnishings, Cutter claimed:

Living room fireplace with handmade dragon andirons and carved lions supporting the crenelated hood, 1901. DSB

Above far right, Fireplace with dragon andirons and carved lions. GG

Below far right, Gothic staircase and newell post. GG

Below, Detail drawing of library fireplace. EWSHS

A number of pieces of furniture suggested for the hall and library run somewhat higher in cost than the Campbell furniture. This is due to the fact that we have submitted pure, rich Gothic design on which there would be much more work, and which would be strictly in keeping with the architecture of these rooms. I would strongly recommend the carrying out of work in accordance with plans submitted, as it, being correct in detail, would always be good no matter how often styles might change. However, should you decide to cut down the cost, less expensive things could be substituted, a partial list of which is attached to estimate.

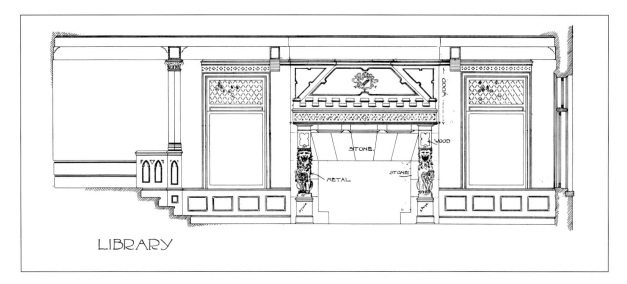

LIBRARY

The hall furniture was expected to be finished with gold leaf decorations, but according to a November 20, 1900, letter, "after the hall furniture was finished, we decided that gold would be no improvement to it on account of the rich shade of brown used."

Most of Cutter's recommendations were accepted by the Stimsons. Sixteen thousand dollars changed bank accounts during the year that followed, a hefty sum in those days.

Cutter sought out and purchased oriental carpets, wallpapers, and upholstery fabrics, sketched and sent to manufacturers drawings for electric fixtures, lanterns, and wall sconces, ordered neoclassical plaster pieces for the reception room ceiling, and selected Italian blue glass tile for the dining room fireplace from "a large number of the best examples of domestic and foreign makes, as being in harmony with the decorations of the room." The main floor was given over to warm finished oak and sycamore with fabric-panelled wall coverings. Cutter made a trip to Seattle in mid-May of 1900 "to assist in getting the colors for interior oak woodwork and exterior timberwork, which are very important to the success of the work." Nevertheless, Cutter insisted that the soft woodwork of the bedrooms and bathrooms be finished in white or ivory paint "as the natural color of fir is not in harmony with any chamber colorings and the white is being used everywhere in preference to anything else."

Not all of Cutter's proposals were carried out. He had sent drawings of a brick perimeter wall and an elaborate Gothic iron arch and lantern for the front entrance. On January 29, he wrote, "This work I think can be done cheaper and in a more satisfactory way in the East." Whatever the reason, the iron piece was never made.

Cutter also tried to interest Stimson in purchasing items not originally in the design but which he was ordering for houses of other clients. On April 7, 1900, Karl Malmgren wrote:

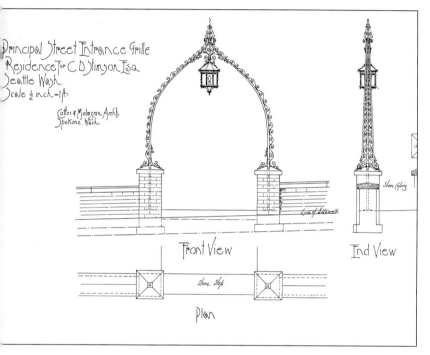

Principal Street Intrance Grille
Residence for C D Stimson Esq.
Seattle Wash.
Scale ½ inch = 1ft

Cutter & Malmgren Archts.
Spokane Wash.

Front View   Ind View

Plan

Cutter's suggestion for a brick wall
and iron arched entranceway.
EWSH

We have just completed a number of large red terra cotta urns for the F. Lewis Clark house, which have turned out very satisfactorily, and as they would be in keeping with the architecture of your house we thought it possible that you might want to have, say four of them made for your large veranda as Mr. Cutter was told by the Denny Clay Co. that they could not make red terra cotta in Seattle on account of the color of the local clay. These urns are quite large and showy, and would cost $10.00 in Spokane."

On June 16, Cutter wrote:

I have just succeeded in getting a very fine and rare suit of Italian armor which is very beautifully etched. It would be very effective and most appropriate in your library. The price is $170. If you should happen to care for it, please let me know at once as Mr. Clark is talking of buying it."

Four terra cotta urns were ordered for the veranda, but the armor does not appear in any contemporary photographs of the library, so it was probably not on Stimson's priority list or was no longer available when he finally made up his mind.

While Cutter did not directly purchase artwork for the house—apart from arranging for the dining room frieze—on May 11, 1900, he wrote a letter of introduction for one Mr. William Morris,

...who goes to your city with a small but very well selected collection of paintings by some of the world's greatest artists. Mr. Morris is well known by lovers of art throughout the country and is recognized as being a buyer of unusual knowledge and taste. he has been very successful in Spokane and should certainly find a place for some of his gems in Seattle homes. I therefore have given him this letter to you, feeling sure that you will be glad to assist him in meeting the right people.

It is not known whether Stimson did, indeed, purchase from Morris or who of Stimson's business associates and friends met and formed a buying relationship with him. But the letter demonstrates the way in which art was routinely purchased and distributed outside of established eastern art markets and that local taste in fine art was undoubtedly formulated based upon the availability of particular artists and stylistic treatments.

Skilled craftsmen who had established working relationships with Cutter were sent to Seattle to do the plaster work, paper the walls, paint the interior, and apply the Lincrusta oilcloth, canvas, and hand painted tapestry friezes that decorated the walls in various rooms. That summer, with nearly everything arriving by rail car, the business of installing all the fixtures, furniture, and draperies began in earnest. Cutter continued to send notes and sketches to Stimson for approval regarding detailing of racks for the wine and cool room, seating in the billiard room, bedsteads, and carpets. On July 6, for example, Malmgren writes,

Enclosed please find blue prints of three different designs in fire sets which we have selected for your dining room, these being numbered first, second, and third choice. We think it rather necessary to have quite ornamental sets for this room and the library, while in the other rooms, they can be quite simple and inexpensive.

The firm even specified the methods of staining the woodwork in the den and billiard room on July 13.

The specifications call for one coat of stain to be wiped for your den and billiard room, which would be sufficient for this climate, but in Seattle, where there is so much moisture, I should recommend brushing on a light coat of raw linseed oil to be rubbed off with cloths. This will be an additional protection to the wood and will cost very little.

Main entrance to the Stimson residence, 1901. DSB

Romanesque vaulted entrance hall with gold painted canvas panels. GG

As with any project so large, some things did not go smoothly and the physical distance between the architect and his client—250 miles between Spokane and Seattle—only made it more difficult to clear up the various order mix-ups, late deliveries, and unacceptable work. Most disagreements arose because of miscommunication with suppliers, particularly carpet manufacturers. Promised goods sometimes arrived much later than planned or, when they did arrive, had to be sent back because they were not the right ones. Cutter was held responsible for the delays, even though his letters tried to explain all of them fully to the clients. Because the letters do not exist from Stimson or Mrs. Stimson, there is no direct evidence of their response to these problems.

While correspondence was his principal method of communication, Cutter also used the telephone—with some frustration. For example, on October 16th, Cutter wrote:

> The telephone was working so badly this afternoon that I was unable to reply to your inquiries which I could only partly understand.

Stimson-Green mansion in a recent
photograph. GG.

It was my hope to have everything about the house completed before your return from the East but through the many bungling errors of the house which is finishing the carpets, I have been unable to do so. After a great deal of correspondence and checking of figures we have finally succeeded in convincing these people that they are to blame for the mistake in the Reception Room carpet and a new one is being made...the stair and upper hall carpet should reach Seattle within a week though we have as yet received no shipping bill. They either overlooked this part of the order or mislaid the data which we sent them, as only a short time ago when we supposed the carpet was in the house, they wrote for more information.

I assure you that I deeply regret the delay and the great annoyance which it has caused you and Mrs. Stimson and can only say that I have done and am doing everything in my power to hasten the completion of the work.

As October dragged on, more things arrived, among them the lining and hinge plates for the gun case and the large screen and fire irons for the library fireplace, manufactured in New York. Through some oversight, wall switches were not installed for the electric lights. On November 5th, Cutter wrote:

Carriage house, 1901. DSB

Stair hall, 1914. DSB

You state in your letter that the chandeliers can only be lighted by screwing in the bulbs. Are the chandeliers not provided with wall switches? It certainly would be very inconvenient to light chandeliers in the way you speak of, and as we never put them in without the switches, it has not occurred to me that they would be omitted.

Please write me further in regard to this matter, stating which chandeliers you have to light in this way, and we will take steps to make correction at once.

As it happens, the chandeliers are turned on by switches built into them at the base which Stimson may have overlooked initially. The wall sconces were not, in fact, connected to wall switches but had to be turned on by turning the bulbs.

Additional furnishings were still being discussed and ordered as late as February of 1901. Last-minute changes also increased the costs, as this November 20 letter relays.

Enclosed you will find a bill from the Western Mill Factory forwarded to us for collection. This is for the carving in wood in your Dining Room mantel and the egg and dart moulding around wainscoting, which was originally specified to be of plastic work. I decided after the work was under way that the plastic work would not do in connection with hard wood, as we had had unsatisfactory experience with it here and, therefore, told the mill people to make carvings instead, at the same time telling them to get your consent to the extra cost for same before going ahead with the work. This, it seems, they did not do and they are now looking to us for settlement of the bill. The $24. is the cost of the work above what plastic relief would have been, and we consider it reasonable, as the work in mantel, particularly, is quite elaborate and very well executed.[6]

---

6. The Stimson-Green house today shows off much of Cutter's handiwork as described in his letters and early photographs. This is the fortunate result of its having had only two families in residence. Very few changes occurred before it was purchased by Historic Seattle Preservation and Development Authority in 1975 and became a designated Seattle landmark. Since then, it has been resold with protective controls that limit alterations to the exterior and major interior spaces. Priscilla Collins, daughter of Dorothy Stimson Bullitt and grandaughter of C. D. Stimson, is the newest owner; she has restored and rehabilitated the house and brought back many of the original furnishings from the Stimson years.

During the period of decorating this house, Cutter had himself been planning an additional office in Seattle to broaden his base of commissions. For the Stimson project he had subcontracted with local architect Charles Bebb to supervise the construction and interior furnishing, paying him two percent of every contract. It was partly the cost of such an arrangement that led him to the decision to establish an office in Seattle. On July 6, 1900, he wrote Stimson:

> We are making arrangements to open offices in Seattle on Sept. 1, as we have found our association with Mr. Bebb to be very unprofitable and realize the necessity of having our own force of men on the spot...We will say nothing to Mr. Bebb in regard to our intentions until after finishing your work and dissolving partnership with him.

In fact, it was March of 1901 before he finally did open an office. In the last extant letter to Stimson on the decorating of the house, dated February 9, 1901, Cutter says:

> We expect to open an office in Seattle within the next two weeks and the man who is going to take charge will go over in a few days to secure a location. After the first of March, I expect to spend a good deal of time in your city, as I realize that Seattle is the coming city of the northwest. Until we send out our notices for reasons which you will probably understand, we do not care to have anything said about the matter. Will ask you to not mention it.

Cutter's work for Stimson was more than satisfactory. Through it and connections he made during his work with Stimson, he was asked to design the Stimson Mill Company building in Ballard. In contrast to the Minor Avenue mansion, this was a simple one-story composition of red clinker brick with round arched windows in the two principal gables and a minimum of ornament— limited to some stone lintels and sills and quoin-like brick treatments at the major corners. In 1903, he was also commissioned to design the prestigious Rainier Club. Over the next decade, while carrying on his Spokane practice, he designed homes for some of the leading figures of Northwest commerce and industry in the Puget Sound area—Thomas Burke, C.H. Clarke, Horace Henry, and Chester Thorne.

From an architectural standpoint, the First Hill house is

Rainier Club designed by K.K. Cutter, ca. 1910. DSB

significant because it ushered into Seattle the English Arts and Crafts style at a scale that had not been seen or attempted before locally. It set a precedent and was a prototype that would be copied and embellished by a host of local designers in the first decade of the twentieth century. These gracious English traditional homes lined and defined the streets in well-to-do neighborhoods of First Hill, Queen Anne Hill, Capital Hill, Denny Blaine, Washington Park, and University Heights.

It was from the Minor Avenue house that domestic life proceeded under Mrs. Stimson's watchful eye. Staff maintained the high standards within the house and looked after the children, giving Harriet Stimson the luxury of time for an active social calendar that included the typical round of calling on other First Hill ladies, having teas and attending club meetings, and actively encouraging—through her verbal and financial support—a variety of important civic undertakings. To these she devoted much of her later life—the development of parks and boulevards, a symphony orchestra, the Cornish School of the Arts, and Children's Orthopedic Hospital.

Harriet Stimson wanted a symphony orchestra to play here and, with the assistance of other women who shared a similar interest, she raised money, located musicians, and made arrangements for the first concert. She even enticed her former music teacher to come out from New York to conduct. She prevailed upon her women friends to go through their husbands' closets and take out their dress suits for the musicians to wear for the concert. It was less important that the husbands would not have "tails" than that the orchestra should make a proper and professional appearance. Harriet even helped plan the opening program, including in it pieces that were especially dear to her. On opening night, surrounded by a community of friends and business associates, the Stimsons listened to Wagner's Tannhauser overture. Harriet sat there with tears running down her face, she was so moved to hear this music. Her husband patted her hand and said, "That's alright Hatty, music is here." [7]

Stimsons on a European trip, 1905. From left, C.D. Stimson, George Gateau, Dorothy, Harriet, Thomas D., and Mary E. Spencer. The car, a Richard-Brazier, was bought in Paris and shipped home. DSB

7. Interview with Priscilla Collins.

THE PUBLIC REALM

C.D., for his part, continued to shuttle from the mill in Ballard to his timber properties throughout the state and to Southern California. In March, 1911, he sold the stock and fixtures of the Los Angeles yard to the Consolidated Lumber Company and leased the property there. By that time, the Ballard mill site, rebuilt in 1890 and operating for years with occasional upgrading of equipment, was showing its age. C.D. recognized that they could only operate it for a short time longer before the Lake Washington ship canal being planned would flood the site. On February 10, 1912, the trustees decided to hire A. B. Pracna, a Vancouver mill designer who had prepared specifications for motors and machinery for the plant in 1906, to draw plans for a new mill.

In addition to the mill construction, Stimson also increasingly involved himself in real estate in downtown Seattle—much as his father had done in Chicago and Los Angeles. He had learned the importance of real estate and began to build a substantial portfolio of properties as a hedge against the erratic swings of the mill economy and to provide a secure future for his wife and children.

He had begun in 1893, at the height of the nationwide depression and with property values at record lows. With $35,000 in surplus funds, he focused his acquisitions on property north of the traditional business district, being convinced that in that sector there would ultimately be the greatest development. He first bought the southeast corner of Second Avenue and Pike Street from the owners. Cornell University had a mortgage of $40,000 on it and C.D. offered $30,000 in cash. He collected rents for a period of three years from the buildings on the site and then sold the property for $100,000. With the proceeds, he made other investments, including the northwest corner of Fourth Avenue and Union Street for $25,000; three lots on the southwest corner of First Avenue and Union for $40,000; a corner at Third Avenue and Marion Street for $22,000; and an interest in the Madison Street Railway Line for $5,000. On the First and Union Street site he had a handsome building built which brought him a high return until he sold it in 1924 for $210,000. The corner at Third and Madison he held for less than a year, selling it for $50,000. When the Madison Street Railway line was sold and incorporated into the city railway system, C.D. received $25,000, five-fold his original investment. The corner at Fourth Avenue and Union Street, which he held, was worth in excess of $600,000 prior to construction of the 1411 Fourth Avenue Building in 1928. [8]

A.W. Spaulding rendering of the hotel building at Westlake Boulevard designed for C.D. Stimson. Special Collections Division, University of Washington Libraries (UW)

---

8. Bayley, 27.

In addition to these purchases, in May, 1903, he bought a small parcel along First Avenue South near South Walker Street in the industrial tideflats area south of the central business district. In 1922, he had a two-story warehouse built there. In July, 1906, he purchased two lots at the corner of Terry Avenue and Union Street—just across Boren Avenue near his home and became landlord of a rooming house, The Altamont. That year, he also made a substantial investment in an area of the downtown that would see enormous growth but which was, at the time, hardly the center of the retail and commercial city.[9]

In November, 1905, Stimson bought a wedge-shaped lot bounded by Westlake Avenue, Pine Street, and Fourth Avenue from Samuel Rosenberg, a Seattle clothes manufacturer who may have used some of the profits from his sale to build his Sorrento Hotel on First Hill. By 1906, Stimson had already engaged an architect, A. W. Spaulding, and a handsome six-story frame hotel and retail building—distinguished by its distinctive shape and multiple bays—was erected on the site. The Plaza Hotel quickly became a landmark because of its location at the junction of two main thoroughfares. In the following year, a seventh floor was added.[10]

Across the street, Stimson developed another wedge shaped property with the six-story brick and terra cotta Triangle Building. For many years, it was leased to Home Savings and Loan. In the ensuing decades, Stimson, on his own and later through various companies, purchased and developed buildings in this north end of town that became the focus of business and cultural life in Seattle.[11]

Above, Warehouse building at First Avenue South and South Walker Street, ca. 1920. SMC

Below, Triangle Building at 4th Avenue and Pine St.

Left, The Plaza Hotel at Westlake , ca. 1910. SMC

9. Information on Stimson properties are extracted from accounting books in the possession of the Stimson Mill Company, Seattle, and property record listings in the Dorothy Stimson Bullitt Archives.

10. The hotel was razed in 1935 for a Bartell's Drugstore. That building was razed and the site is now Westlake Park.

11. These properties, including the Coliseum Theatre and 1411 Fourth Avenue Building, are discussed in Chapter 6.

At the Willows with friends, ca. 1905. Stimson is second from left. SMC

COUNTRY GENTLEMAN

While his First Hill home might have seemed a refuge from the business world, it in fact functioned as a social gathering place for business associates and the focus of concerts, dinner parties and receptions for out-of-town guests. In the game room or the billiard room, over after-dinner cigars, Stimson and his associates discussed their expectations for the city and their shared ideas for investing in Seattle's future. It was here that the idea for The Highlands development probably took shape, and for the General Insurance Company (now Safeco Insurance Company).

But the First Hill house was not the only place where Stimson and his associates mixed business and pleasure. In 1904, C.D. developed a poultry and pigeon farm in Kirkland, had a rustic lodge built, and frequently went out with friends for several days of hunting and birding. He called his country manor the Willows, and it appears to have been a great escape for him from the formality of Minor Avenue. It also was offered to friends like Henry Hadley, the conductor of the Seattle Symphony, as a quiet retreat for weeks at a time. In the Willows guest book, grateful recipients of Stimson hospitality frequently turned to poetry to express their thanks, as in this April 30th, 1910 somewhat forced effort.

April 30th – 1910.

The Willows for mine
At any old time
You can't beat it rain or shine;
A good log fire
A voice to inspire,
And plenty of good old wine.

Now here's a toast
To a genial host
In the good old April time.
May he always have luck
And plenty of duck —
And now we've finished our rhyme.

Wm. B. Clayton.   Henry Hadley
Mabel C. Clayton   Marguerite Reudru
                    Katherine Bentley
                Richard Bentley

Sample page from the Willows guestbook, April 30, 1910. Henry Hadley was the conductor of the Seattle Symphony. DSB

C.D. Stimson at the Willows, 1910. DSB

The Willows for mine
At any old time.
You can't beat it rain or shine;
A good log fire
A voice to inspire,
And plenty of good old wine.

Now here's a toast
To a genial host
In the good old April time.
May he always have luck
And plenty of duck—
And now we've finished our rhyme.[12]

It was not at all unusual for a man of Stimson's position to have country property as well as a town house. The lifestyle that C.D. established for himself—the town house and the country house—was quickly adopted by his brother Frederick. Frederick, in addition to having a grand and lavishly decorated home built on Queen Anne Hill, did himself become lord of an exquisite country manor.

---

12. The Willows guest book, Dorothy Stimson Bullitt Archives, unpaginated.

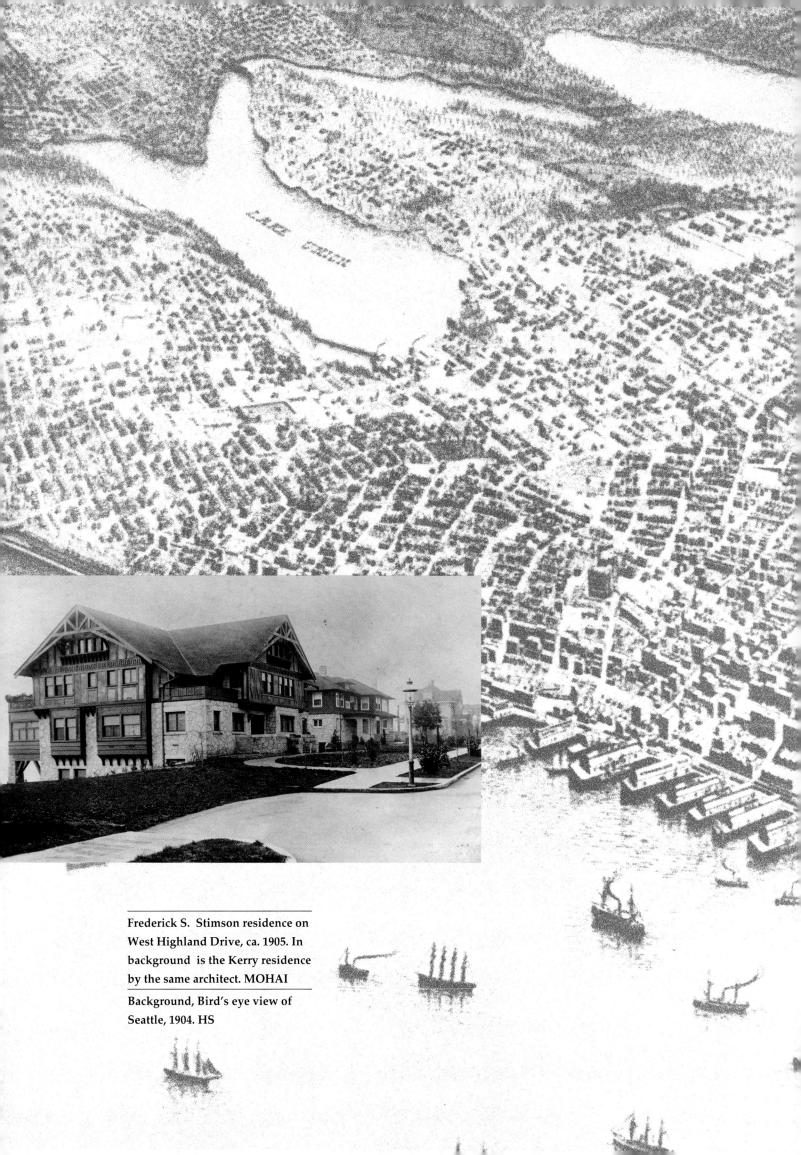

Frederick S. Stimson residence on
West Highland Drive, ca. 1905. In
background is the Kerry residence
by the same architect. MOHAI

Background, Bird's eye view of
Seattle, 1904. HS

Chapter 4

THE FREDERICK STIMSONS OF QUEEN ANNE HILL

Frederick S. Stimson, ca. 1900.

Shortly after the Minor Avenue home became the family seat for C.D., Harriet, and the children, brother Frederick bought property on West Highland Drive with a dramatic view of the harbor and began planning an equally substantial house for his family. His brother's home impressed him; the English style suited him, as it did his neighbors, A.S. Kerry, Harry Whitney Treat, and C.H. Black. All four gentlemen sought an architect in whom they would have confidence. It was no coincidence that Stimson and his neighbors chose Charles Bebb.

While Kirkland Cutter clearly intended to leave Charles Bebb behind as he set up a Seattle practice, Bebb himself was probably feeling less than satisfied with an arrangement whereby he was responsible to Cutter. By 1900, he had amassed impressive credentials and skills as an independent designer.

Bebb was born in Surrey, England, in 1858 and educated in London at King's College. He studied engineering at the University of Lausanne in Switzerland and had been employed for five years as an engineer by the Cape Government Railroad in the building of the Capetown-Kimberley Railroad in South Africa.

Birdseye view of Seattle, 1904. HS

He arrived in the United States in the 1880s and found employment for five years as Construction Engineer with the Illinois Terra Cotta Company. He joined the office of Adler and Sullivan as Supervisor of Construction in late 1888. His first view of Seattle came in 1890 when he was sent to arrange for construction of an opera house designed by the firm.

Seattle was still undergoing its transition from a tent city after its 1889 fire into a quality downtown lined with brick and stone buildings of substance. A group of local businessmen, undoubtedly impressed by the reviews of Adler and Sullivan's Auditorium, which opened in December, 1889, sought the firm's assistance to create a sufficiently grand and impressive symbol of the new city. The project faltered during the recession that year; by 1893, the entire country was facing depression. Nevertheless, Bebb was impressed by the energy and growth potential of the fledgling city, and with hardly any work coming to Adler and Sullivan, he chose to relocate to Seattle and try his luck.[1]

For five years at the Denny Clay Company, Bebb's Chicago experience with terra cotta and fireproofing materials led to great growth for the company. During 1894-95, he was one of the founding members of the local chapter of the American Institute of Architects. After completing his role for Cutter at the Stimson residence, in 1901 he partnered with Louis Leonard Mendel (1867-1940).[2]

THE CITY HOUSE

Bebb first became acquainted with C.D.'s brother Frederick during work on the Minor Avenue house. By the time Frederick began thinking about a substantial home on the southwest slope of Queen Anne Hill, the firm of Bebb and Mendel had already attracted attention for their particular brand of English medieval residential architecture so popular elsewhere in the country at the turn of the century.

For the Fred Stimsons, the firm designed a distinguished three-story home, its stucco and half-timbered upper floors rising above a fortress-like stone ground floor punctuated by shingled square bays. The cross-gabled roof with overhanging eaves terminated in decorative truss vergeboards. At the rear of the house, facing south to views of Puget Sound and the city and supported by its own stone pillars, was a large, shingled sunroom with wrap-around windows.

Charles Herbert Bebb

Unlike Cutter, who maintained almost total control over his projects by insisting upon completing all the interiors down to the design of furniture and furnishings, Bebb and Mendel appear to have preferred recommending top notch interiors firms to complete the shell in appropriate style. In the case of the F. Stimson house, the William A. French Company of St. Paul, Minn., was commissioned to oversee the interiors. Bebb subscribed to the belief so frequently echoed by Cutter that the best craftsmanship and the widest variety were still only obtainable in the East. French was already known in Seattle circles, as he was at the time engaged in completing the interiors for Mrs. Anderson, the wife of an important Northwest lumberman and in the same social circle with both Harriet Overton Stimson and her sister-in-law, Nellie Clark Stimson.

1. Jeffrey Karl Ochsner and Dennis Alan Andersen, "Adler and Sullivan's Seattle Opera House Project," *Journal of the Society of Architectural Historians* XLVIII, no. 3, (Sept. 1989): 223.

2. Some of their most notable commercial work includes Schwabacher Hardware and the Hoge Building. In 1914, Bebb and Carl Gould formed a partnership. Their legacy included the campus plan and many of the buildings at the University of Washington, constructed beginning in 1916.

F. S. Stimson residence in a recent view. GG

Entrance foyer and stairhall. GG

An extensive correspondence between Mr. and Mrs. Frederick Stimson and William French from June 1903 through the following September indicates the degree of detail which such a project entailed, particularly when each of the principal rooms was to be outfitted in such a way as to properly evoke a particular historic period and style, ranging from Elizabethan to Italian Renaissance to Indian, Persian, and English Arts and Crafts.[3]

The firm presented bids on June 15, 1903 for decorating the house that listed the various treatments. The first floor hall would be decorated with white oak friezes, the ceiling finished in oil, stippled, then decorated in Elizabethan design around the beams. "Portieres" (draperies in each of the doorways) were to be of orange-red crinkled tapestry with leather applique and borders in Elizabethan design. In the billiard and adjoining smoking room, rich, red burlap panels on the lower wall would be complemented with upper walls decorated in an Indian design. Portieres and over curtains here were to be of canvas with applique and heavy embroidery in Indian designs and

3. Letters and inventory lists from William French to Mr. and/or Mrs. Frederick Stimson, Dorothy Stimson Bullitt Archives.

soft silk curtains "in suitable design and coloring to correspond with the decorations and furnishings."

The main floor reception room was to be panelled in Circassian walnut with fine Italian Renaissance tapestry and finished with silk galloon. The upper wall would have a frieze with "rich decoration in the same style, to be done on canvas and put in place." The beamed oak ceiling would be covered with canvas and done in oil color with a soft stipple finish. In the drawing room, yellow poplar walls in Georgian design would be combined with upper walls covered in green silk damask and the ceiling finished with "rich plaster relief moulded decoration...the ceiling and cornice to be finished in rich old ivory shade, to correspond with the woodwork." Four pairs of portieres of plain green velvet decorated with rich Kensington embroidery and lined with sateen would complement the wall colors. Silk curtains with moss silk edging were suggested for the east windows. The oak dining room walls would have tapestry panels and its ceiling would have "a heavy Old English plaster ornamentation." The portieres for this room were to be of blue old English Reps with tapestry borders to correspond with the tapestry wall hangings.

The six bedrooms were each to be decorated differently, to evoke English, Indian, and Persian environments. The decorator's penchant for the popularly promoted English styles is apparent in his suggestion of William Morris pattern "Myrtle" paper in Chamber 1 and the use of other English botanical papers—roses, tiger lilies, tulips, and birds—for other rooms. The finest imported linens, silks, sateens, embroidery, and tapestry were to be used.

The basement hall wainscotting would be covered with

Above, The classically inspired mural in the reception room was painted by California artist Arthur Matthews. GG

Below, The billiard room, decorated with Navajo designed stenciled walls, rugs, and Indian baskets, 1906. Washington Architect (WA)

Drawing room. View toward
dining room, 1906. WA

green Japanese leather, the upper wall hung in green burlap, with a frieze decoration and tinted ceiling. The hall led to a ballroom with a stage at one end and a hearth and retiring room at the other that would be covered with Japanese grass cloth. These rooms are the only two in the house that show Charles Bebb's direct influence. Their rich Sullivanesque plaster work and the design of chandelier and sconces are a radical departure from the more traditional treatments on the two upper floors.

Furniture suggested by the firm included richly carved, English-styled dining room, oak table and cabinet for the central hall, Chippendale drawing room chairs and sofa, an Elizabethan desk on the balcony at the head of the stairs, and mahogany, oak, and enamel painted furniture for several of the bedrooms.

The estimate for all these decorations was $6,535, with the woodwork costing $10,485, and Irish and Scottish rugs and carpets costing an additional $2,700. The total estimate came to $25,000—a substantial sum in 1903.

By November, and continuing through January, William French corresponded frequently (and separately) with Mr. and Mrs.

One of the upstairs bedrooms
decorated with William Morris
floral papers, 1906. WA

Stimson—he at his Globe Building offices, she at their suite of
rooms in the Washington Hotel. He arranged for one of his foreman, Mr. Siebert, to come out and install the various woodwork,
fabric, and furnishings as they arrived in Seattle. Numerous changes
occurred. And French was always on the lookout for appropriate
pieces for the house.

On Nov. 28, for example, he wrote:

> I have taken the liberty to forward a very beautiful rug for
> your reception room which I found lately in New York. It is a rare
> piece and the coloring is particularly fine for your room. I therefore
> considered it an opportunity not to be lost as I may not find another
> nearly as good in style, quality, and color...I have not purchased it
> however but had it sent on with the understanding that if it was not
> decided upon it would be returned within a few days.

A later letter indicates that they kept the rug.

In notifying them of the woodwork, he wrote,

Elizabethan ornamental band
above Ionic pilaster in oak
panelled hall. GG.

Carved oak strapwork balusters
distinguish the handsome
staircase. GG

The last shipment of your interior wood work will be sent early next week and I want either Mr. Siebert or the other man to arrive about the same time so as to push the work along as fast as possible...I expect to be out there when the wood work is far enough advanced so that I can inspect it properly which will be either late in December or early in January.

His detailed letters during December reveal his rethinking of color schemes and combinations. On December 12, in treating the drawing room, he wrote, "I do not feel quite satisfied with some of the materials for furniture covering which I showed you when there. The room seems to need a little more variety and depth of color." He proceeded to suggest a darker material for the Chippendale Divan, for a high-back divan and chair—in all cases to material costing $4.00 a yard more than that originally suggested. For a triple back seat and chair in the hall, he also selected a more expensive material, but justified it thus:"I am very anxious to have your house as handsome as possible not only with a view of pleasing you but believing it will be of benefit to me with your friends in the future."

Later on in the same letter, referring to the reception room woodwork being installed, he commented, "The carving is pronounced by experts here to be as fine an example of Italian Renaissance work as they have ever seen in this country or abroad."

By Jan. 9, the woodwork had been installed, although French made reference to the dampness of the house and his concern that it might have an adverse effect on the panelling, causing it to shrink as it dried out. In fact, he was covering himself in the event that they would complain later. As he put it, "If such shrinkage should occur in the future you will understand that it was neither due to poor workmanship or green lumber."

After spending several days in Spokane on another project, French arrived in Seattle about the 20th of January and inspected the work there. Letters written in Seattle on Jan. 28 and 29, 1904, indicate that he shopped locally for a dining room rug and found something appropriate. He also prepared an estimate for lighting fixtures ($2,815.); additional cushions and rugs ($516.50); more furniture, this time for the reception room, drawing room, hall, ballroom, and rear porch ($3,067); and assorted small accessories, all to be shipped from St. Paul.

The Stimsons were still at the Butler Hotel in April, select-

ing from samples of damask for ballroom furniture. Two furniture cars were shipped out from St. Paul with everything but the ballroom and the reception room furniture, which French immodestly noted "is undoubtedly the finest thing we have ever done, both the design and the workmanship being exquisite." On April 21, he mentioned a Tabriz rug for the dining room ($1,600.) An April 30 bill shows the original estimate and the later add-ons totalling $30,327.32.

French accommodated them with small purchases for the house even after they moved in. On May 25, he "purchased a very handsome Tiffany desk set which I am sure will please you. It goes perfectly with your room being in green glass and antique verde metal...I have a very handsome dull old copper set, the general character of which would be nice for your hall...This is Arts and Crafts work in beaten copper with the ornament done in colored enamels...the pedestal for your reception room is finished and was shipped with the carpets by Northern Pacific freight."

Another billing, on May 28, indicates purchase of additional Elizabethan tables and chairs, an octagon hall table, an oval table for the retiring room, some screens, mirrors, vases, and jardineres, and windows. In his letter, he states, "The sketches of Italian jardineres and flower stands represent a few pieces which I obtained of an Italian and the ones with the lion's head can be seen

The ballroom shows the influence upon Charles Bebb of Louis Sullivan's principles of ornament. GG

The Sullivanesque ballroom has plasterwork painted in rose and light green. GG

The sunroom at the south of the house, 1906. WA

in Mr. Bebb's office. They are very nicely modeled and good in color besides being quite unusual." One of the screens, with thistle ornament, "seems especially appropriate to go in the room with the Sullivanesque ornament and would be decorated handsomely on a light cream Japanese grass cloth....I am on the lookout for a good lamp for your drawing room and some nice suitable Italian pieces to ornament your reception room."[4]

4. The Stimsons sold the home to move permanently to Woodinville. Since that time, the home has had two other owners. As a Designer Showhouse, a significant number of inappropriate changes occurred to wall and ceiling surfaces and original lighting fixtures. Nevertheless, the French Company woodwork and trim mouldings are generally intact and the Sullivanesque ballroom, while needing restoration, is also intact.

THE COUNTRY HOUSE

Frederick and his wife began searching for property in the country for a summer home and weekend retreat only a few years after the house in town was occupied. They found acreage in the Sammamish valley near the farming community of Woodinville — north of The Clise estate in Redmond and C.D.'s own hunting retreat, the Willows. Stimson proceeded to have an estate house built about 1910, possibly by local architect Fred Sexton. He had worked in Tacoma in the 1880s and 1890s and had done a substantial amount of institutional work in Ballard, where the Stimson mill was located. Among his projects had been the Webster School and two log-and-river-rock chalets in the Craftsman Style for Annie and Homer Russell in 1904 (5803 and 5727 8th Ave. NE).[5]

The house was oriented toward a formally planted parterre garden. It was a handsome two-story Craftsman-styled lodge with

Aerial view of Hollywood Farm, ca. 1915. WSHS

Hollywood Farm dairy truck, ca. 1915. WSHS

5. Interview with Dennis Alan Andersen.

At Hollywood Farm. Left to right: F.S. Stimson, Frank O. Lowden, former governor of Illinois, farmer and cattle breeder, and Elbridge A. Stuart, founder and president of Carnation Milk Company. WSHS

a broad central gabled roof, overhanging eaves supported by decorative open brackets, and two symmetrically placed, cantilevered gabled bays. Three sets of French doors fronted on a trellised veranda. This permitted easy flow of traffic into and out of the main living room, which was dominated by an enormous river rock fireplace. Many bedrooms and sleeping porches on the second floor accommodated the extended family during weekend visits and summer retreats.

The house became the showpiece of his Hollywood Farm; other buildings included a four-car carriage house, a superintendent's house, greenhouses, and numerous agricultural buildings. Here Stimson introduced many innovations, including a modern laboratory for scientific testing of the day's milk production, a powerhouse, an ammonia plant to produce ice, trout ponds and extensive greenhouses where his wife Nellie raised roses for sale. From the nearby main line of the Northern Pacific Railroad running through the Sammamish valley, a siding was built which terminated in front of an ice cream parlor on the farm.[6]

On Oct. 10, 1914, the *Town Crier* carried a detailed description of the property in an article entitled "A Little Journey to Hollywood." It took readers by car from Seattle "to the edge of a great valley."[7]

Below for several hundred feet was to be seen the snaky road twisting among the trees. Further on, spacious green fields and pasture meadows stretched away to the distant opposite heights. In the west stood a great low manor house, burnished gold beneath its wide roof, with other picturesque attendant buildings clustered around about. There were spacious terraced gardens, in which even from the heights we could distinguish the glow of many colored flowers and the wink of tumbling water. Beyond lay huge barns and greenhouses, among which towering silos and the stacks of a power-house brought to the spectator's fancy the thought of a medieval fortified grange. On the hill side moved countless spots of black and white, the fat herds of the manor. And crowning the opposite summit we discerned the outposts of the domain, a cluster

6. "Stimson Develops Sammamish Ranch," Real Estate Section, *Seattle Post Intelligencer*, Sunday, May 7, 1911.

7. *Town Crier*, Oct. 10, 1914, 6-7.

of snow white houses and sheds which strongly suggested the presence of innumerable poultry.

Descending the steep hill with cautious brakes, the car came to a great iron gateway and passing this, swept up a fine boulevard beneath slender concrete lamp posts, each surmounted by a single great globe, to the courtyard of Hollywood Farm, the famous estate of Fred S. Stimson, capitalist, lumberman, country squire, and owner of one of the finest herds of Holstein-Friesians in the United States. Four years ago, this great homestead, comprising nearly a section of land in the rich black valley of the Samamish Slough, was an unpromising jungle of logs and tangled second growth. Today it is as perfect an estate as the West can show.[8]

---

8. The farm was acquired in 1975 by Chateau Ste. Michelle which has placed additional buildings on the site, razed a number of dairy buildings, and maintained the house and some of its outbuildings.

The symmetric form of the main residence works in harmony with the formal gardens it fronts. WSHS

TERRA COTTA POTS

IRON
BALCONY

EL. OVT.

22 / 6 6

24 / 5 5¼

NICHE

SVN DIAL

CEMENT
SEAT

EL. OVT.

26 ½ / 8

24 / 6 6

South façade of Norcliffe fronting
the entrance drive. DSB

K.K. Cutter's elevation drawings
for Norcliffe in The Highlands.
EWSHS

BREATHING SPACE

Seattle was no longer a rough and tumble mill town with aspirations in 1908, as it had been when Stimson and his family arrived in February,1889. The population had increased to nearly 300,000, and areas of the city that had been cleared timber land in 1900 were by now platted and built upon. First Hill was getting crowded. New homes, apartment buildings, and hospitals were infringing on what had been a quiet and somewhat exclusive residential community less than a decade before.

Seattle's boosters were so pleased with themselves and the city that had replaced the forested hillsides that planning was afoot for a major exposition to show the world it had come of age. Modelled after the great World's Columbian Exposition of 1893 and other grandiose celebrations, this one was to focus attention on Seattle's choice location for the exploitation of resources in Alaska and the Orient. The fair was to be a model example of architecture and planning, and its developers looked outside Seattle's local community for its lead architects and landscape designers. The Olmsted Brothers of Brookline, Massachussets, having already made connections during their preparation of the Parks and Boulevard plan for Seattle, were chosen. They were to devise a scheme for the fledgling University of Washington campus site in preparation for the buildings of the Alaska-Yukon-Pacific Exposition. The Olmsteds' presence in the city did not go unnoticed by C.D. Stimson and his friends, who had grand ideas of their own.

Developing the Highlands

The main lounge, Seattle Golf Club, the Highlands, ca. 1910. SMC

K. K. Cutter's 1908 drawing of east elevation, The Seattle Golf Club. EWSHS

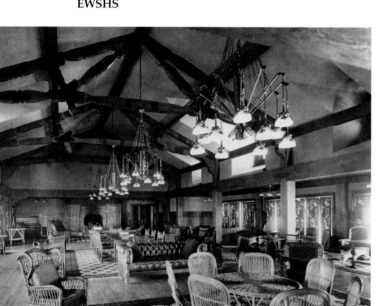

The old Seattle Golf Club located in Laurelhurst was feeling the pressure of real estate developers. It had never been a large course, with only nine holes, and access to it was commonly by boat. A new site was needed to accommodate an eighteen-hole course that would be suitable for its members. A specially appointed committee at the club examined on foot and on horseback all available tracts of land from Three Tree Point north as far as Richmond Beach before it decided on a 380-acre tract of undeveloped land three miles north of the old city limits—85th Street—near the shores of Puget Sound. Part of the tract was sculpted by John Ball into the new Seattle Golf Club grounds, and the remainder was sold as residential lots to club members. The Highlands would offer breathing space, privacy, and recreation within a short commute of the central business district.

C.D. Stimson made the first step. He either purchased outright or arranged for options on the land. Records show that at one time the

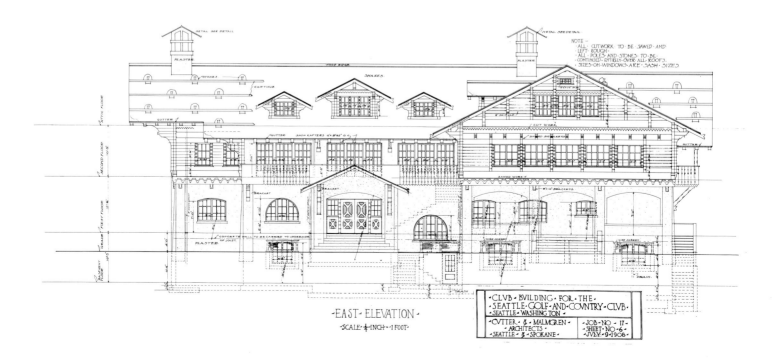

- EAST- ELEVATION -
-SCALE-¼-INCH-1 FOOT-

·CLVB·BVILDING·FOR·THE·
·SEATTLE·GOLF·AND·COVNTRY·CLVB·
·SEATTLE·WASHINGTON·

·CVTTER·&·MALMGREN·	·JOB·NO·17·
·ARCHITECTS·	·SHEET·NO·6·
·SEATTLE·&·SPOKANE·	·JVLY·9·1908·

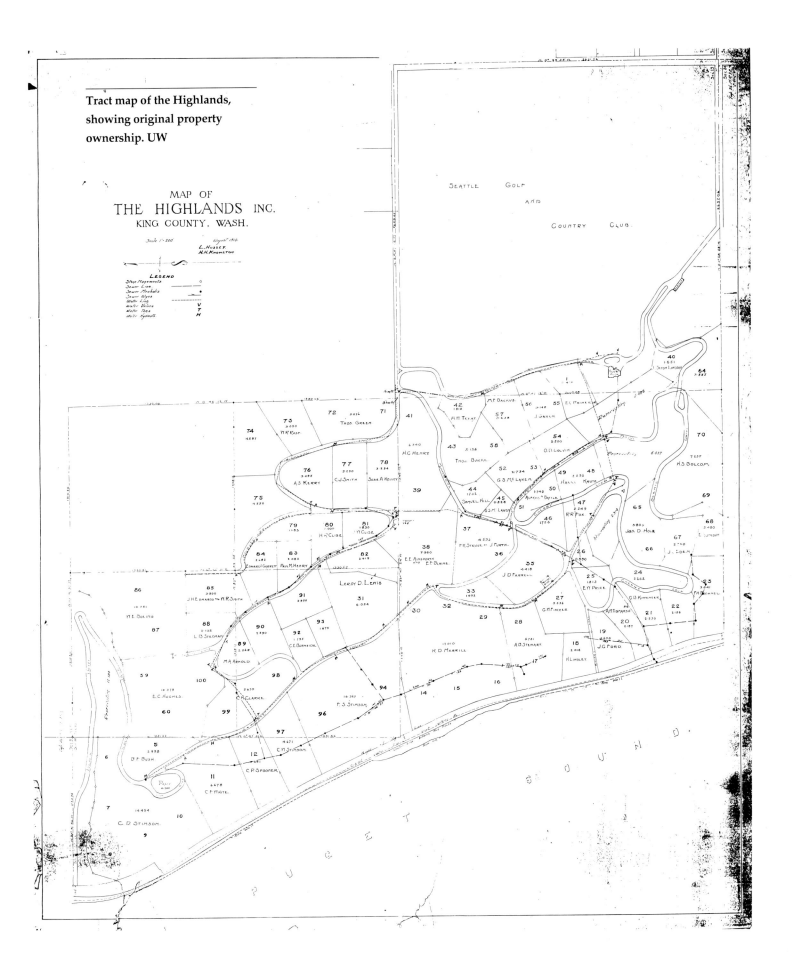

Tract map of the Highlands, showing original property ownership. UW

entire tract now known as the Highlands was in his name.[1] Articles of incorporation were drawn up and the Highlands charter was signed on Apr. 24, 1908 by C.D. Stimson, A.S. Kerry, F. K. Struve, E. F. Blaine, C. J. Smith, H.W. Treat, and C. D. Stedman. The first meeting of the new club was held at the Stimson home on Minor Avenue with all twenty-two of the original members in attendance. C.D. Stimson was elected president and continued in that role for 11 years.

The concept of the Highlands was remarkable. While the idea of an exclusive community bordering a golf course seems commonplace now, in 1908 this breadth of vision was unusual. It proposed master planning of a residential community that preserved native-growth forest by restricting where building could take place and by prohibiting tree cutting without permit from the Highlands board. In most cases, houses could not be seen from the roads, and they were developed with an appreciation of and a great respect for the hilly, forested, topography and its naturally occuring fir, maple, madrona, salaal, and Oregon grape. Views of Puget Sound were an important attraction of the properties, but many of the plats lacked views and their homes were set in landscaped clearings within the northwest forest. The later additions of a chapel and a school, courtesy of Horace Henry and C. D. and Harriet Stimson, turned the housing development into a more cohesive community. It was the perfect marriage of wealth, power, design skill, and commitment to preserving natural surroundings.

The first survey and topographical map of the tract was made by A.S. Downey, a civil engineer.[2] The Highlands Board gave the map to the Olmsted Brothers with the instructions to lay out roads and plat residential tracts and park areas. Ultimately, the Olmsted firm received a large number of commissions from individual tract owners to do site planning, garden design, and even to design outbuildings and pavilions.

Choice of residential tracts was determined by lottery, and Judge Thomas Burke drew Tract #1, the most desirable view property. It didn't take long for C.D. to maneuver a trade -the property he had drawn nearer the golf course in exchange for the Burkes' bluff property. The first home built in the Highlands was that of Mr. and Mrs. W.A. Tidmarsh. From then on, distinctive homes by some of the region's and the nation's finest architects were constructed.

The beachfront below the Stimson's bluff property, ca. 1930. SMC

---

1. Bayley, 65.

2. Downey married Emma Collins, daughter of John Collins. The Downey's home adjoined the White property (later Greenway, the home of Dorothy Stimson and A. Scott Bullitt).

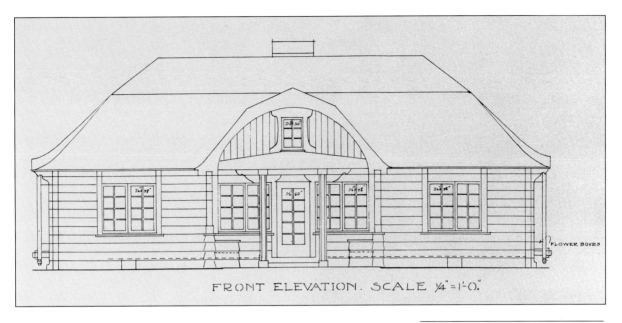

FRONT ELEVATION. SCALE ¼"=1'-0."

Elevation drawing for the cottage, 1909

Kirtland Cutter, having been hired (probably through Stimson's efforts) to design the new clubhouse, was also the obvious choice for Stimson's most ambitious private residence. But it would be several years before a permanent home arose on the the Stimson site.

Instead, C.D.'s son Thomas took the initiative and designed a cottage in a clearing on the site so that family and friends could comfortably gather there whenever they could escape the city. On Feb. 13, 1908, he wrote to his sister Dorothy, then aged 16 and visiting in Los Angeles,

> Yesterday, while at the Willows I made some measurements which I think will be useful in building our house. I found that we have 22 feet x 9 feet for two rooms upstairs, mother's room and a bathroom. The porch at the Willows is 46 feet x 7 feet. I think we had better make our porch 7 feet wide, don't you?..The largest bedroom in the lodge is 9 x 13. I think your room will be 12 x 12. [3]

With his ideas sketched out, Thomas went to Cutter to help him finalize the cottage design and prepare working drawings.

Stimson's newest project, Norcliffe in the Highlands, was replacing the Willows by 1908 as the family retreat. Stimson found ample opportunity to go off on hunting trips with friends who had property elsewhere in Puget Sound so he rarely visited the Willows, and Thomas was left in charge. By October of that year, the family

3. Letters from Thomas to Dorothy Stimson, Feb. 13, 1908 and Oct 14, 1908. Dorothy Stimson Bullitt Archives.

was looking to extricate itself from the Willows. Thomas wrote his sister on the 14th, "Did I tell you that I think I have found a man who wants to lease the ranch and buy all of the poultry. Is that fine. You don't know how much trouble and expense this old place is."

By October, Thomas' cottage was finished, and Harriet Stimson wrote to her daughter, then at Mrs. Dow's School in Briarcliff Manor, New York.

I am writing at your little desk in the cottage at the Highlands. Brother and I came out alone yesterday. Your father went off on a hunting trip expecting to return this evening. Brother and Robert have been planting shrubs all the morning. Rhododendrons and laurels and a few azaleas. I hope they will all grow and I think they ought to as the soil is good and they have been very careful in the planting. [4]

The rustic Arts and Crafts cottage fit comfortably into the forest setting. Its hipped and gabled roofs were sheathed in cedar shakes and the side walls were covered with dark-stained shingle. There were ample multipaned windows with white frames and mullions. The dining room windows at one end of the house had multipanes forming a segmental arch above four operable windows. The main entrance porch was protected by the large gabled dormer with a semi-round arched bargeboard that housed a second-floor bedroom. At the rear of the house was the kitchen and servants' quarters.

When Cutter designed Stimson's first home, in 1899, he was unknown in Seattle. But the distinctive Minor Avenue home may have prompted the Rainier Club commission of 1903. Its influential members took note of him, as they dined at Stimson's house and conducted their business in front of the massive hearth in the main lounge of the club. Thomas Burke, C. H. Clarke, Horace Henry, and Chester Thorne relied upon Cutter's design prowess for homes in Seattle and southward to American Lake. For the Seattle Golf and Country Club of 1908, Cutter chose the Swiss chalet, one

The cottage at Norcliffe. DSB

4. This and following excerpts are taken from the Stimson letter files in the Dorothy Stimson Bullitt Archives.

of his favorite styles. Indeed, he had adapted that rustic style years earlier for his own chalet home in Spokane.

Stimson asked the Olmsteds in 1909 to evaluate his Highlands property and to suggest landscape, roadways, and the ideal location for the main house. Their projections show a winding driveway from the main road skirting the west front of a large house roughly planned in an H form. The house was placed at the upper part of the site to take advantage of views. Pathways followed the rolling topography through various lawns, formal and informal garden spaces, and native forest. Cutter's 1913 house plan differed slightly but was built in approximately the same location suggested by the Olmsteds.

In her Oct. 25, 1908, letter to Dorothy, Harriet Stimson says:

> We cannot seem to get hold of Mr. Cutter to have our plans charted and it is very annoying but we like him so much better than anyone else that I think we will simply have to wait for him. I do not care so much about commencing the house as I regret the loss of time—in regard to shrubs, trees, etc., but we have about decided to go ahead with the planting of the bank at the point according to Mr. Olmsted's suggestion. The new road is still progressing rather slowly and the old road is almost impossible. It is so cut up by the heavy loads of stone which are being drawn over it, we were almost stalled in the mud there last night.

On Feb. 8, 1909, Thomas wrote to his sister:

> Mr. Kerry and Father are working hard to get the council to pave the road. It will cost a lot of money and the City doesn't want to pay for it. But all the Golf club are working for the road and it will eventually go through I think...The club house will probably be finished by the last of March. It will certainly be a dandy. There well be two open fireplaces down stairs one in each end of a large room. There is one fireplace upstairs. Porches are stuck on all over. Fourteen rooms are up stairs for people who wish to stay there all night...The road is not quite finished as yet, but will be by the end of next week.
>
> Mr. Cutter thought that a Dutch Colonial style would be better for Mother's house than any other. His idea was to build it in this shape [drawing shows a three section segmental arch]. You see with the house built this way it would not spoil so much of our view. The house would be built close to the ravine.

As it turned out, the Dutch Colonial was dropped in favor of a less-confining English country architecture which was tagged

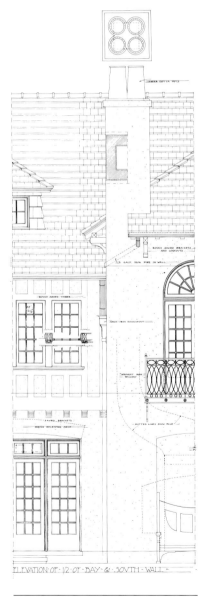

Elevation of south wall, Norcliffe. EWSHS

"modified Mission" in several published descriptions, probably for its stuccoed exterior and generous use of colored tile.

C. D. Stimson gave Dorothy a progress report on March 24, 1909:

> Improvements are going slow at the Highlands tho' I think by time you return all roads will be macadamized. Our plot of ground laid out, a garage and stable built, and a house started, also roads through tract finished. Golf Club house looks very well and I think it's going to be a popular place this summer. Fairgrounds are being completed and all will be ready on June 1st for the opening and it's all going to look very pretty and really be a creditable show. Yacht is being put in commission. Willows and all horses are fine.

In a letter to Dorothy on May 27, 1909, Harriet noted:

> We have tried so hard to have the Garage commenced out at the Highlands, we have had two sets of plans drawn, the second came only yesterday but we have decided to accept them so your father was to telephone today and ask Mr. Cutter to get out the working plans at once. It may be commenced before you get home, but not much more than that.

NORCLIFFE RISES ON THE BLUFF

The main entrance door, Norcliffe.
Mary Randlett (MR)

Norcliffe was to be a very different house from Cutter's first Stimson effort. The Minor Avenue house had been limited by its site. It was a large house for turn-of-the-century Seattle, but it was not designed for entertaining in the style that had become the custom. Its rooms were limiting, too, partly as a function of their historicism. There would have been no reasonable place for the display of the great many lithographs, etchings, and engravings that Mrs. Stimson was acquiring. The rooms were all quite formal. There was no place for casual conversation or patios and sunrooms for occasional pleasant weather. There was very little outdoor space for children's play. The Stimsons were seeking a change, and Cutter was given the chance to create a house suitable for large parties and intimate dinners, balanced with formal and informal spaces, with comfortably scaled rooms and simple finishes that would be a good background for furnishings and art. He would also be called upon to exploit the views from the site—something with which he did not have to concern himself on Minor Avenue. Norcliffe was already isolated and private. There was no reason to draw heavy draperies to shut out the sun and curious passers-by.

Norcliffe may have been inspired by the English-country-house style promoted by Charles Voysey and Sir Edward Lutyens at the turn of the century and interpreted quite loosely by Cutter and other residential architects for the newly evolving upper classes. Cutter's earlier residence for Louis Davenport in Spokane, a sprawling stucco manor house, shows some of that influence. Furthermore, the dramatic setting of the Highlands property, among the trees with views of the water and Olympic Mountains, was not lost on Cutter. At Norcliffe, the ease and casual good manners of the English country house were married to the pitched roofs, stucco and tile facades, loggias and arcades of the Mediterranean villa to create a home that suited both the damp and cool Northwest winters and the sunny and comfortably temperate summer months. It bore strong affinities to southern California Mission revival homes.

Visitors driving to the house passed a small gate lodge and followed a road through the woods that broke into a clearing of lawns and rhododendrons. Dropped off at the porte-cochere, they made their way to the main entrance along an arcaded cloister in the courtyard fragrant with heliotrope and potted orange trees. Two major chimney stacks were massed in the front of the house with a garden seat at the bottom and a balcony above accessed from French doors in an inset arch. The flanking bays were half-timbered at the

The house sits amid cherry trees, rhododendrons, and azaleas in a clearing in the Northwest forest. Much of the Olmsteds' work and that of Harriet Stimson has been altered by changes to the terraces adjacent to the residence. MR

Leaded glass windows in pocket doors leading to the ballroom. GG

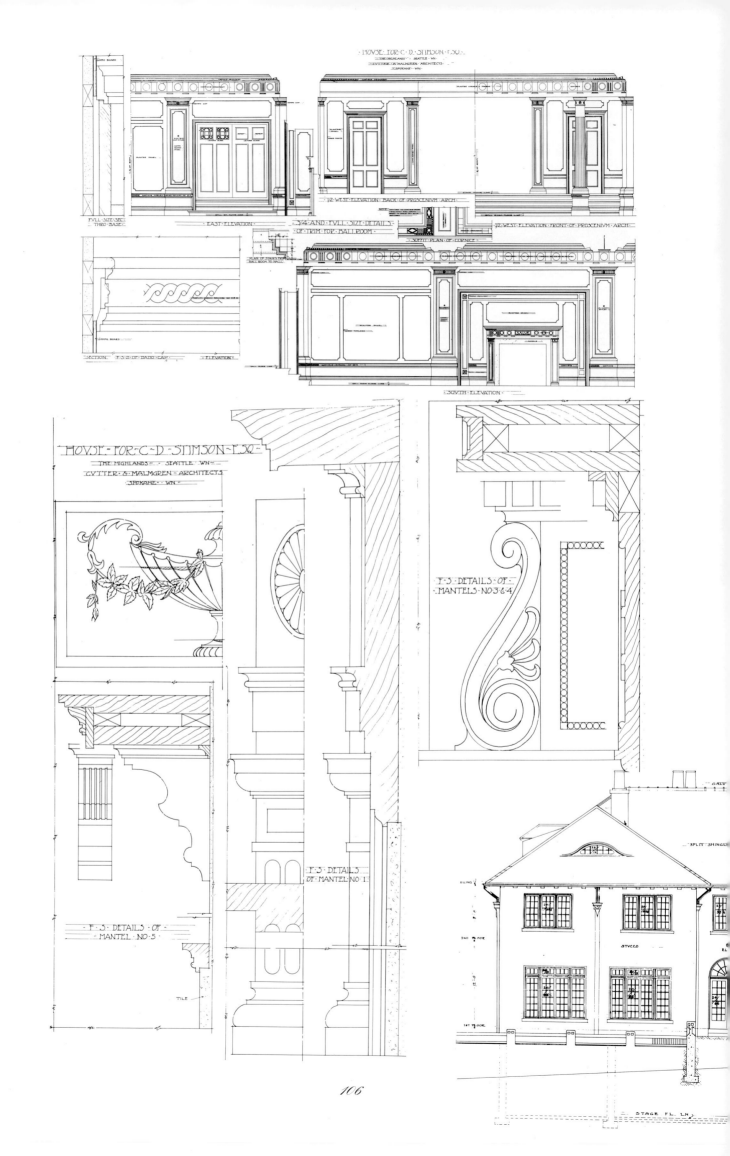

HOVSE · FOR · C · D · STIMSON · ESQ ·
THE HIGHLANDS · SEATTLE · WN ·
CVTTER · & · MALMGREN · ARCHITECTS ·
SPOKANE · WN ·

FULL SIZE SEC
THRO BASE   EAST ELEVATION   3/4 AND FULL SIZE DETAILS   1/2 WEST ELEVATION BACK OF PROSCENIVM ARCH
                                            OF TRIM FOR BALLROOM   1/2 WEST ELEVATION FRONT OF PROSCENIVM ARCH

1/2 WEST ELEVATION BACK OF PROSCENIVM ARCH

SOVTH PLAN OF CORNICE

SECTION · F·S·D· OF DADO CAP · ELEVATION

SOVTH · ELEVATION ·

HOVSE · FOR · C · D · STIMSON · ESQ ·
THE HIGHLANDS · SEATTLE · WN ·
CVTTER · & · MALMGREN · ARCHITECTS ·
SPOKANE · WN ·

F·S· DETAILS · OF
MANTELS · NO · 3 & 4

F·S· DETAILS
OF · MANTEL · NO · 1

F·S· DETAILS · OF
MANTEL · NO · 5

TILE

STAGE FL. LN.

106

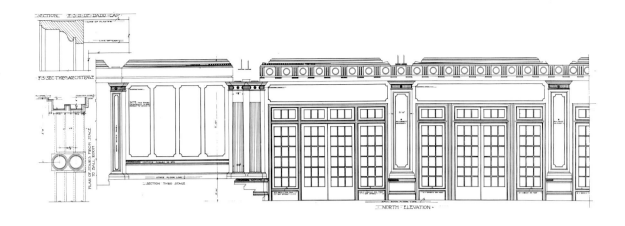

- NORTH · ELEVATION -

Clockwise from below right: north
elevation; south elevation;
fireplace and mantel details;
interior elevations for ballroom,
including fireplace and French
doors. EWSHS

- NORTH · ELEVATION -

-HOVSE · FOR · C · D · STIMSON · ESQ-
- THE · HIGHLANDS · - · SEATTLE · WN -
- CVTTER · & · MALMGREN · ARCHITECTS -
- SPOKANE · · WN -

107

The wisteria covered arcade leads from the driveway to the main door. MR

A second floor bedroom has a balconied window facing onto the principal courtyard. GG

second floor. Rows of French doors from the living room led directly into this courtyard. The paths of the courtyard gardens were bricked, the stuccoed railings detailed with colored and incised tiles, and vines and tall flowering plants added color to the ensemble. Pathways led to the various garden levels, each marked by cement balustrades so that each level had its own personality and distinction. A curious, undulating roofed cupola crowned the central stair, and the pitched roofs were punctuated at intervals with various square and eyebrow dormers, all of which added to the charm and idiosyncratic qualities of its mix of formal and vernacular design elements.

While there is no correspondence relating to the initial planning of the house, documentation exists for the building period of 1913-14.

Ledger figures indicate that by July 30, 1914, the cost of work on the residence, including furnishings, had risen to a high of $99, 993.19. By the time the Stimsons moved in, their costs had probably escalated from there.

An article written by Kirtland Cutter for *Pacific Builder and Engineer* in the Dec. 11, 1909, edition reveals the attitude toward domestic design which he directed toward work at the Highlands site.

Modern domestic architecture has sought to assemble the ideals of every age and nation, and adapt them to the enormously expanded tastes and requirements of modern civilization. It has sought, not only to make the home beautiful, comfortable and practical, but also to make it an influence that shall enter into the building of the lives that are largely spent within its walls...The grounds, the trees, the flowers—even the surrounding landscape—are all integral parts of the home and must be determined before the plans for the house can be made...The lines of the house also must harmonize with its surroundings. If the house is on a gently sloping knoll, the roof must have a very low pitch to conform to the surrounding contour.

In planning the house itself, the main results to be obtained are spacious living rooms (and every part of the house to be lived in at all the time)...Modern domestic architecture has forever banished two elements supposed to be necessary in the oldtime house—the musty smelling parlor or "spare room," and the back door. The breakfast room should have plenty of sunlight and the principal chambers should be on the leeward side of the house. Whenever possible, there should be a great fireplace; it cannot well be too generous in its proportions. Sometimes these fireplaces are ten or twelve feet wide and four or five feet deep, with open chimney and brick seats inside each end, where one may sit on cold nights by the crackling fire and toast his feet to his heart's content. Not only are these huge fireplaces of the greatest value for ventilation, but nothing adds so much to the cheer of the home.

The finish and details of the rooms should be plain rather than ornate. Modern good taste has well-nigh banished varnish in house finishing...Last, but far from least, come the furniture, the decorations, the draperies, the pictures, the books, the bric-a-brac and what not. Many an architect has gone out of a house, into which he had put his very soul, discouraged and dismayed at the havoc which that dangerous triumvirate—the housewife, the decorator and the furniture dealer—had made of all his work. Where the architect had left soft lines and exquisite harmony, he finds glaring discord and impossible combinations.

In the furnishing of a house, two or three fundamental rules

One of two strapwork decorated beams in the living room. GG.

Fluted columns and neoclassical moulding characterize the ballroom decor. GG

A cast stone garden fountain is the focal point of the courtyard adjoining the ballroom. MR

One of a number of Moravian tile panels that decorate the stucco exterior walls. MR

should be held to as sacredly inviolable. One is that the furnishings throughout should be as rich and elegant as may be, but never pretentious; and as far as possible, every article should mean something. Another is that nothing should be out of key. Every room should be so arranged that, upon entering it, one may take up the details one by one."[5]

At Norcliffe, Cutter used a large variety of tiles from various manufacturers to enhance and give special character to each of the rooms and to the facades and perimeter walls of the house. He ordered from William W. Kellogg, Inc., a local distributor of "mantels, tiles, grates, marble and bronze, fireplace fitments, art pottery, and garden ornaments." He chose Moravian glazed tiles in assorted designs and colors that were inserted in the stucco bulkheads and posts and rails around the house and eight Moravian glazed panels to embellish the ground floor facades. He also ordered two peacock panels, as well as numerous other colored tiles for exterior work.[6]

At Norcliffe, Cutter insisted that each fireplace be different, as he had done in the earlier home. He designed and had Kellogg provide dressed stone for the living room mantel, incised with the date of construction (1914), Rookwood tile for the dining room facing and hearth, and a special design in Batchelder tile for the library facing and hearth. The ballroom fireplace was faced in Fleur de Peche Marble, as was the adjoining lounge area. The various bedrooms upstairs each had distinctive fireplaces faced with Volkmar tile in two tones of blue, tan Grueby tile, English Lustre, decorated Medmenham facing, old rose Rookwood, and blue gray dull glaze with black and white ceramic decoration.

In addition to these decorative tiles, quarry pavements were laid for the breakfast terrace, the veranda, the sun porch, and ambulatory spaces. Red brick detailed the pathways and formed borders for the terraces and walkways. For the courtyard adjoining the ballroom, Cutter ordered a cast stone garden fountain complete with lustre glass mosaic basin—for the then princely price of $300. Adding the cost of labor to the cost of the materials, the Stimsons were billed through their contractors, the Johnson Brothers, for $4,449.15.

5. "Architecture in the Northwest", *Pacific Builder and Engineer* (Dec. 11, 1909):484-5.

6. An incomplete collection of order forms from manufacturers and suppliers, inventories, and letters from K.K. Cutter to the Stimsons are in the Dorothy Stimson Bullitt Archives.

While hopes seemed high that the house would be started in 1909, it would not begin in earnest until 1913 and, according to the personal accounts of Mrs. Stimson, took her constant attention. Indeed, while the Minor Avenue house had been more C.D. Stimson's project, Norcliffe was Harriet's. Every day or two during that and the following year, she would spend two hours journeying to and from the site to oversee the various decisions that had not been resolved in Cutter's drawings. Having a designer whose main practice was in Spokane and who did not promptly respond to her letters and calls led to considerable frustration.

A series of letters from Cutter's office dated June 14, 1913, through Apr. 10, 1914, documents the working drawings phase and construction of the estate. They cover the disposition of everything -- bathroom fixtures, to mouldings, to wallpapers, and carpets. It was an expansion of the First Hill process and, at least as it appears from Harriet's letters to her daughter Dorothy, then studying in New York, this time the house was designed to Harriet's specifications. C.D. simply acquiesced and paid the bills as they arrived. It was, after all, his wish to please her and it is clear that K.K. Cutter understood that in his dealings with the family.

Cutter's letter of June 14, 1913 let C.D. know that revised plans for the foundation and basement were being sent, along with "prints of full size details for all of the basement frames in order to

The wisteria-draped arcade is reminiscent of a medieval cloister. MR

Edwin Ivey peeks out from the newly completed playhouse, built by Thomas Stimson on the Norcliffe grounds, 1921. UW

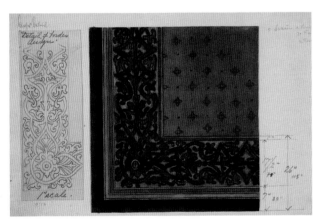

Library with Bachelter tiled fireplace. Mrs. Stimson's print collection and fine bound books are displayed on the wall at right. DSB

Cutter's water color sketch of Renaissance styled ornamental border for library carpet. DSB

avoid delaying any of the work....Everything is working out even better than expected and the house is going to be a beauty."

On June 21, Cutter forwarded blueprints from the working drawings and requested comments, including feedback on whether the Stimsons wanted tile wainscoting in the bathrooms or might prefer Cutter's own preference, enamel over plaster with a six-inch sanitary tile base and tile floor. He also recommended freestanding pedestal type porcelain tubs, which Mrs. Stimson, in a later letter, had obviously decided against in favor of an "engaged" tub. Again on June 25, the firm wrote to Stimson hoping "soon to receive the reply as the working drawings are being developed rapidly and the different matters pertaining to the work should be decided as promptly as possible as they come up."

Later letters did not address the principal living spaces to any extent; instead, they were more concerned with efficiency items, such as the arrangements of the vacuum cleaner, refrigerating machines, and the dumbwaiter, and whether to design drawers or rollers for storage of table cloths in the pantry. "In some cases the cloths are folded once through the center and laid in drawers, while others prefer rollers, which, of course, are rather awkward and require a good deal of space for the very large cloths."

On July 26, 1913, a two page letter to Mrs. Stimson discussed her concerns about plate warmers, closet fittings, the ice

machine, and dust. Cutter reassured her of the proper steps being made to ensure that her new home would be beautiful and efficient. He maintained that his details for the ballroom and indeed for most of the house were

Living room, showing carpets here and in the hall designed by Cutter, 1914. The table at left is from the Minor Avenue home. DSB

> ...made just as simply as possible, and in designing the mouldings, I have constantly kept in mind the matter of cleaning and dusting, which has so much to do with the livable qualities of the house.
>
> For instance, the plaster cove for bath rooms is merely drawn mouldings in plaster, easily and cheaply executed, and with no member on which dust can rest...
>
> You will find the details of the main rooms on the ground floor are also simple. Where wainscoting is shown, the panels are flat and

Aerial view, Norcliffe, ca. 1925. In
foreground at the edge of the bluff
is the tea pavilion. DSB

the mouldings low. In the Living Room, in order to shorten the effect
of the two main beams, we have shown a plaster corbel with some
ornamentation, and have also shown a flat carving on the fireplace
beam, as well as in the Dining room, in order to relieve it from the
otherwise rather severe effect. In the ball room we have shown a
classical treatment with a cast plaster frieze and double columns on
the stage back of which the curtains can be draped. The walls of this
room are panelled by applying small wood mouldings so that it can
be easily decorated in shades of French gray and ivory, or in fact, in
any colors desired and I feel that it will make a very beautiful room
in quiet good taste.

We have specified for the finish throughout selected vertical
narrow grain fir to be enamelled, which I feel will be much more
attractive and satisfactory in every way. We are finishing most of
our best houses in this way and have never had any complaints
about the care of the light woodwork, which, of course, would have
a perfectly smooth surface and an egg shell gloss. With this treatment any kind of furniture or any consistent mixture of styles can be
successfully used, as well as any color combination for decorations
and draperies.

Cutter ends this letter, "I am greatly interested in your
house, as I consider it one of the very best things that I have ever

done, and am anxious to have everything entirely satisfactory to you in every part of the work."

By mid-September, the house and its details had started to fill Harriet Stimson's daily calendar, as the following excerpts demonstrate. The letters shed light on how building construction was accomplished and how frequently or infrequently the architect was available on the job. They also show the extent to which contemporary books about design and decoration, such as Elsie De Wolfe's *The House in Good Taste,* influenced American women in shaping their family environment. While the letters reflect the period, they also reveal how universal and timeless are the issues surrounding the building of houses.

Sept. 18: I went out to the Highlands today—the house showed some progress-they were putting in floors and partitions in Hall, Living Room and Kitchen part and it begins to look as though it would really be a house some day. The cook in the garage decided that it was too lonesome for her after all and she is leaving tomorrow.

October 16: A man from Mr. Cutter's office is to be here tomorrow and we expect to be out with him all day. Thomas has been of such help to us in the plumbing and heating plans. We almost entirely abandoned Mr. Cutter's plan and put an expert to work on them in Mr. Shack's office and brother has spent a great deal of time with them until they seem very perfect—but time will tell as to that.

Nov. 26: This afternoon the rain poured down in sheets, but brother and I went in the car to Mr. Shack's office and again went over the heating plan for a couple of hours—from there we went over to Crane and Co's and decided on a few extra things in connection with the plumbing fixtures—and hope that all such things are settled for the present. I was out to the house yesterday afternoon and am going to spend the day there tomorrow—to see to getting the Bulbs in and some other planting.

Dec. 14: I told you of Mr. Cutter's preference for grey and pink for your rooms. We were talking it over when he was here and found some tile with a little pink in it which was very dainty and seemed suitable for your fireplace and of course would be a little newer than the blue but we found some pretty blue tile so if you prefer the blue we can use the grey and pink somewhere else. Mr. Cutter leaves next week for New York and will be at the Vanderbilt for a month or more, and you can call him up and talk colors over with him if you

Stucco walls were backdrop for Harriet Stimson's lush flower garden. DSB

The formally planted patio and walkway adjoining the ballroom. DSB

West facade, showing sunroom and covered veranda off the library. DSB

wish. Mr. Dawson from Olmsted Brothers arrives today. We are very glad to have him here as the grade of the road is not yet satisfactory.

January 20: I went out to the Highlands again yesterday and spent most of the day. It sometimes seems a very futile way of spending my time but I cannot arrive at very satisfactory conclusions when I only see it on paper. Things look so different when I see them actually before me.

January 26: It is such a slow process that sometimes I feel like staying away for a whole week just for the pleasure of realizing that it has grown, but am always afraid of something going wrong. We had a terrible storm yesterday and last night, pouring rain and a seventy-five mile gale. I couldn't sleep thinking of the danger to the trees at the Highlands, but no harm was done except to blow down some limbs that were already dead.

Feb. 15: I have been reading Elsie DeWolfe's book *The House in Good Taste* and have enjoyed it so much in fact it has come to be almost a text book with me. I have always admired her interiors and think she more nearly approaches my idea of what a home should be than any other decorator I have ever known anything about, and am trying to work out the upstairs rooms (excepting yours) along the lines that she advocates at the same time trying to utilize old carpets and furniture where they fit in best. It is very interesting but very absorbing and as I am perfectly well aware that I have no particular ability in that direction I am all the more anxious.

Feb. 22: I can readily see how it would be quite natural for you to think that I am attaching undue importance to things connected with the house but it has been and still seems to be my particular business in life for the present. And I am so anxious that it should be in good taste and every inch of it for constant use to leave the windows open and let the sunshine in, without feeling that something is being spoiled. I am sure to make mistakes but hope they will not be irreparable. It has been difficult to have Mr. Cutter so inaccessible. Many little things come up which I know nothing about but have to decide as your father has troubles enough of his own this winter, and I do not like to bother him. It is good to have brother back and know that he will look after the machinery end of things.

March 1: Both you and brother seemed so out of sorts with (Cutter) that I thought perhaps it was better for me to communicate directly with him, which I have always found very satisfactory. You know his errand East was principally to furnish the Davenport Hotel in Spokane, from the decorations to the table linen and silver, really everything, which as it is the best Hotel in the Northwest, meant hundreds of thousands of dollars expenditure, and I expect that it was quite natural that he should attend to that first. I think it will all come out right though the thing I have feared was that the assortment selected for us would be the repetition of something in the Davenport Hotel. For that reason I have read and studied everything that I can find on the subject so that I can reject or combine in a different way the various schemes which he may send. While we want the house so simple in treatment and so particularly liveable, those very things increase the importance of just the right color scheme and treatment.

March 14: At last the package from Mr. Cutter arrived yesterday and your tile came this morning. I think they are very soft and pretty and am taking them down to Mr. Kellogg right away. Most of the things I like very much indeed but the yellow linen for Room No. 6, I am certainly not educated up to. I think that he must have forgotten that it has a southern exposure. I do not dislike the plan for the dining room wall covering though it is certainly very unusual and rather bold in design and coloring.

April 5: The bathtubs arrived on Thursday but two of them

Harriet Stimson. DSB

**Dining room, 1914. Here too, the
Minor Avenue furniture was used.
DSB**

**Cutter's water color sketch of
dining room carpet with Chinese
inspired floral borders. DSB**

were cracked in transit and I am afraid cannot be used. We may have to take whatever we can find here to replace them rather than wait for new ones. The tile for the roof has not even been shipped yet...Mr. Cutter's drawings for the electric fixtures have finally arrived and for the most part are very good. They cannot be finished for six weeks.

November 19: Two of the rugs arrived today, one for the dining room and the other for the library. The living room rug seems to have been side tracked somewhere this side of New York, and may come along most any day. They make the rooms seem very much more furnished and I think them a great improvement. The music room is at last finished and the draperies hung, electric fixtures in place and makes a very plain but pretty room.

The house was near complete by April, 1914, and Cutter was still engaged in the decoration of the rooms. While his task was made somewhat simpler than it had been in the earlier home (there were no hand-painted medieval friezes, gold painted canvas ceilings, Flemish carved oak bookcases, balusters, and mouldings), nevertheless, the business of selecting appropriate lighting fixtures, carpets, and draperies was considered, by Cutter, to be of sufficient importance that he should take the time to make recommendations. On Apr. 10, 1914, he wrote:

Our office sent Mrs. Stimson several days ago the Spokane Drygoods Company's prices on materials which I selected while in New York after a thorough search for the best things for the draperies and chair coverings for the various rooms in your house. If they are satisfactory to Mrs. Stimson and she does not succeed in getting better prices on them from Frederick and Nelson, they can be furnished through the Frazer-Patterson Co. either by the yard or they will figure on making and hanging the draperies and covering the furniture.

The price by the square yard on the special Austrian hand tufted rugs of $13.40 which I gave Mrs. Stimson was for the least expensive grade the manufacturers will guarantee, and which I feel sure would be entirely satisfactory from an artistic and service standpoint. This price includes the special clipping of design, to give it an embossed effect of $2.50 per yard which, if omitted, would reduce the cost to $10.90.

I have had sufficient experience with the Bollentin & Thompson rugs to satisfy me of their superior merit and of all the special orders placed with them our clients have in no case been disappointed.

Mrs. Stimson did indeed request estimates from Frederick and Nelson for the hand-tuft rugs in living, dining, and hall, as well as for Wilton carpet for the second hall and stairways. Three were prepared in March and April, based on several samples; the final estimate ranged from $3,182.65 to $4,053.35.

For the Minor Avenue house, Cutter himself designed most of the fixtures and had them made to conform to his sketches; for Norcliffe he recommended lighting fixtures readily available from a Midwest manufacturer or from a Portland company.

Stair hall, 1914. The bench, chest, and clock in Flemish gothic style were made for the Minor Avenue house. DSB

Cutter's watercolor sketch for hall carpet. DSB

While in Chicago, I took up the matter of electric fixtures with the Wilmarth Co., whose designer is one of the very best in the country and their designs for your house, I think are very good, though you may be able to do better in prices on the stock fixtures with local concerns. I have also asked the J.C. English Co. of Portland to submit designs which will be forwarded in a few days for comparison as to artistic merit and prices.

In studying out color schemes together with fabrics, I have striven to bring things together in a simple and harmonious way consistent with the quaint and unostentatious architectural treat-

Above, The Highlands School, designed by David Myers for the Stimsons. MR

Below, Florence Henry Chapel in the Highlands, 1911. MOHAI

ment of your house, and to secure good and serviceable materials at bottom prices, and so that you will receive the benefit of the best discounts.

My charge for this work including all further assistance I can give in the matter will be $500.00, and which I think you will find very reasonable, considering the time and study involved and its importance in relation to the Architectural treatment, together with the saving in cost of the various parts of the work. As the expense to me was heavy and my bank balance is in the red, I would greatly appreciate a cheque from you at this time, if convenient.

This last paragraph hints at an ongoing problem Cutter had holding on to money, despite his substantial fees for such large estates. Ultimately, his management of finances got the better of him, and his financial woes reached a point where, at age 63, he had to quietly close up shop in Spokane. In 1923, he relocated to Long Beach, California, to begin his career anew. With years of practice in working cordially and cooperatively with the most important figures in the Pacific Northwest and his familiarity with the Highlands, it took little time to make the right connections with newly rich oil barons. He helped plan the exclusive development of Palos Verdes Estates, designing award-winning Mission Style stucco and tile homes for the wealthy (Norcliffe may well have been a prototype for this work), and a beautiful bathhouse facility fronting the ocean.

In an interview with the *Spokesman-Review* shortly before he left Spokane, Cutter summed up his efforts of thirty years:

Never have I completed a commission without wishing I could do it all over again and do it much better. Some of my first homes here—like the Glover home or the F. Rockwood residence—have been treated very kindly by the vines which have covered their early faults. I always built to achieve the effect of age, at least to make the building fit into its surroundings to look as if it had grown there and had not been superimposed. I have been criticized for that quality many times, but when the wind and weather complete the work I start, the owners are usually reconciled to the idea.[7]

---

7. *Kirtland Kelsey Cutter: The Collection*, 57.

WINTERING IN THE SOUTH

While Northwest families relished the brilliance of summer, with its long hours of sunlight, mild temperatures, and access to the mountains and the waters of the Sound, it was another story during the winter. The rounds of golf, the garden parties, and the yachting excursions on Stimson's 75-foot yawl-rigged sailboat *Olympic*, the 65-foot power boat *Gloria*, and finally the 90-foot motor launch *Wanda* slowed. It was customary for families of means in Seattle to seek periodic escape during the damp, rainy winter months.

One of the more popular destinations was southern California. From the 1880s on, beach resort hotels on the order of the Coronado in San Diego and the Monte Vista in Monterey catered to the wealthy. By the 1920s, with the development of the rail system, particularly the tourist oriented Sante Fe and Southern Pacific, and the beginnings of automobile touring, everything from luxury hotels to bungalow courts sprang up to meet the demand of the "snowbirds" from the east and the midwest and the waterlogged northwesterners.

For C.D. and Harriet Stimson, who had shared Christmas at the family house on Figueroa Street and had frequently taken picnic

Stimson's yawl, the Olympic, ca. 1910. SMC

Above, The 90-foot motor launch Wanda. DSB

Below, The Stimson family at the Seattle Hunt Club, ca. 1915. SMC

excursions out of town into the orange and lemon groves, including Willard's Eagle Rock ranch, the allure of southern California was well known. When they considered spending part of the winter there, they moved into one of several commodious hotels designed specifically to cater to winter visitors. As it became a yearly extended trip, they established themselves more permanently in one of the many comfortable guest homes built on the grounds of the Huntington Hotel in Pasadena. They called their winter hideaway Clovelly. It consisted of two attached residences; the Stimsons occupied Clovelly West, their friends and travelling companions, Mr. and Mrs. Baer, occupied Clovelly East.

Henry Huntington, a railroad millionaire with a penchant for real estate development, had built the Huntington Hotel as one of a number of amenities to attract tourists to Pasadena. But the cottages ringing the grounds were appealing to those who, like the Stimsons, wanted a second home without the maintenance worries. In a contemporary promotional article, the cottages' appeal was fully exploited:

> Detached and semi-detached cottages, bungalows, and villas constitute one of the charms of life at Hotel Huntington. Surrounded by lawns and gardens, placed in the varied topography of the spacious hotel grounds, many of them overlook the wonderful

views of the San Gabriel Valley. Many families who have fallen under the spell of Pasadena have established houses at the Huntington as their permanent homes. Other families, whose home establishments are in the East, or the Midwest, or the North, or Canada, nevertheless engage their villas at the Huntington by the year, and as time goes on, spend an increasing amount of time at the Huntington yearly. Still other cottages, villas, and apartments are available to seasonal guests.

There is a disarming individuality to each of these Huntington guest homes, varied in treatment and fitting harmoniously with its surroundings. In the lush Pasadena climate, under the expert monitoring of Huntington gardeners, beautiful flowers, trees, and shrubs embellish the settings, giving a homelike atmosphere. Yet all those who settle themselves comfortably in this environment have at their beck and call all the facilities and services of one of the great hotels of the world. Hotel Huntington, standing majestically on its own slopes of Oak Knoll and with these houses and bungalows nestling prettily on the flanks, constitutes a delightful little community of itself. Here, one may enjoy all the metropolitan urbanities and semi-country life at one and the same time.[8]

A picture postcard view of the Huntington Hotel and its beautiful grounds. UW

Clovelly West, the Stimsons' Huntington Hotel cottage, Harriet Stimson with three of her grandchildren, Nona and Douglas Stimson, and Harriet Bullitt. SMC

---

8. Promotional brochure, Dorothy Stimson Bullitt Archives.

Background, Fourth Avenue elevation, The Stimson Medical Building by Howells and Albertson. UW

Right, Roman arched terra cotta facade of the Coliseum Theatre has laurel leaves, wreaths, and urn. MR

Below, Olympic Hotel under construction. Metropolitan Theatre is visible at left. DSB

Chapter 6

BUILDINGS FOR GROWING CITIES

Lower Second Avenue, Seattle ca. 1910. HS

C.D. Stimson moved his office from the Ballard mill into the newly built White Building at Fourth Avenue and University Street in 1909, as if to acknowledge the family shift from lumber to real estate interests. For the next twenty years, his view from the curving corner windows would be of cranes, steel, and concrete; the sound of construction would filter into the office as the buildings of Metropolitan Center and his own 1411 Fourth Avenue Building took shape. He would be an important catalyst for all of these projects.

The C.D. Stimson Company was incorporated on Feb. 8, 1909, by C.D. and Harriet Stimson as a private investment enterprise. With their children, Thomas Douglas and Dorothy Frances, as minority stockholders, C.D. intended to facilitate the eventual transfer of his holdings while giving them the opportunity to learn the business first hand. C.D. and Harriet conveyed all their jointly owned properties to the new company. They consisted largely of real estate and high-grade securities, among which were the following: the Altamount Block at Third and Broadway in Los Angeles; Belmont, Boylston and Union Street properties; the First Avenue and Union Street property; the Second and Lenora Street corner; the Colonnade at First Avenue and Pine Street; the Fourth Avenue and Union Street property; the Bagley Addition to the City of Seattle on the north side of Lake Union; the First Avenue and Lenora Street property; the Tide Flats Building on First Avenue South near Walker Street; land in Richmond Beach; the Willow Lodge at Lake Sammamish; the Hanford Orchard at White Bluffs; vast farmlands near Tracy, California; the Lake View Acre Tracts on Lake Whatcom; and the Stimson brothers property, consisting of tracts of land in King, Snohomish, Whatcom, Lewis, Thurston, Island, and Homestead counties. Additionally, stocks were signed over to the company from the: Metropolitan Building Company, Alaska-Yukon-Pacific Exposition, Sammamish Boom Company, South Seattle Land Company, and Wenatchee Development Company. Thomas Stimson conveyed property belonging to him on Harvard Avenue and Pike Street. C.D. deeded, in trust, the Flatiron Building on Westlake Avenue at Pike Street and the Triangle Building, also on Westlake Avenue.[1]

Meanwhile, Harriet Stimson was directing her energies to making Seattle a more hospitable place for the arts. As her household became virtually self-sufficient, the duties of the house in the hands of responsible help, her time was available to devote to causes she cared about.

Harriet Stimson loved music and was frustrated that there was virtually no opportunity to hear "good" music in the city. Because she was reputedly the best pianist in Seattle for some time, she was in demand as the accompanist to great singers who toured the Northwest. Geraldine Ferrar and other equally renowned operatic and musical stars came to tea at the Stimsons.

As a key member of the Musical Arts Society, a group of women musicians, she helped raise the monies needed to underwrite the symphony orchestra. A close friend of Nellie Cornish, Mrs. Stimson continually provided leadership and support to establish and maintain the Cornish School of the Arts on a firm financial basis. She was also active in the Seattle Garden Club and Children's Orthopedic Hospital. Harriet's interest in bringing culture to Seattle was supported by her husband's financial resources. In matters of business, he was in charge. But when it was a question

A meeting of the Board of Trustees for the Seattle Symphony. Left to right: Lester Turner; Mrs. A.S. Kerry; Mrs. E.C. Hughes; Mrs. A. B. Stewart; Mrs. C.D. Stimson, President; Mrs. Frank R. Van Tuyl. In addition to her cultural involvements Harriet Stimson was a leader in social welfare, founder of Visiting Nurse Services and Seattle Children's Home. DSB

1. Bayley, 59-61.

of design, art, music, or literature, he deferred to his wife.

While Harriet was broadening Seattle's base of classical entertainment and supporting Cornish's training program in the arts, C.D. was directing his energies toward "popular entertainment" in a manner that might have surprised him since his major forms of entertainment revolved around golf, horseback riding, automobile touring, and yachting. It had been largely through his initiative that the Highlands community became a reality, and his favorite architect, Kirtland Cutter, gave the Seattle Golf Club its splendid new facility. But there were equally long-lasting developments in Seattle's downtown. In 1914, he invested in two memorable projects, the Natatorium, known as the Crystal Pool, and the Coliseum Theatre. For both of these buildings, he hired a relative newcomer to the architectural community but one on whose potential Stimson was willing to gamble—B. Marcus Priteca.

THE COLISEUM THEATRE

In 1913, when the Highlands home was well enough along to start planning the move, Stimson made it known that his First Hill residence was for sale. John M. and Abbie Frink approached him with the suggestion of a trade— the house for a half-block of land in downtown at the corner of Fifth Avenue and Pike Street. Stimson agreed, and the C.D. Stimson Company acquired the property on Aug. 7, 1914, by assembling a package that included the Minor Avenue residence (valued at $70,000), assuming two mortgages in the amount of $133,500, and making a cash payment of $36,500. As it turned out, Frink

B. Marcus Priteca at work in the on-site office during construction of the Coliseum Theatre, 1915.
MOHAI

was in ill health, and although he owned the house for several months, he never lived in it. Instead he or his widow sold it to Joshua Green later that year.

Stimson and Joe Gottstein discussed at length the idea of a theatre on the downtown site. Gottstein, 24 years old and fresh out of Brown University, recalled years later that he had originally gotten involved in the Coliseum venture because Washington State had gone dry, putting his father's liquor business "on the rocks." The theatre was his first major business enterprise.

Stimson agreed to build the building ($200,000) and furnish it ($65,000). The Coliseum Company would lease and operate the theatre at a cost of $100 a day or $36,000 a year for the first twenty years and $42,000 a year for the remaining five years of the lease. At the expiration of the twenty-five years the building and furnishings would come back to the Stimson family.

With a foresight that anticipated a growing market, Stimson and Gottstein chose to build a theatre exclusively for film. The Liberty Theatre, opened in 1914, was similarly built for film only. Although the Coliseum was built without a conventional stage— the handsome proscenium arch framed the silver screen and the back wall of the theatre— plans for future development into an opera house would have been feasible with expansion into the then-vacant half-block to the north. It was Stimson who hired B. Marcus Priteca to design the theatre.

A letter dated Mar. 7, 1915, from Harriet Stimson to her daughter in New York, hints at the importance of the project for C.D., coming as it did during a particularly low period in his business ventures.

This by E.C. Williams & Bro N.Y.

> Your father is very happy about it as he feels that for the present it is a splendid business proposition. As to the future it may be worth much more than the rent they pay twenty years from now. But none can tell, the growth of a city is always a matter of speculation and the lessees are taking a much greater risk than we as the town may take a turn and grow to the north rather than up Pike Street in which case we get our income just the same. Of course there is to me the objection that to build the building and furnish it we must go still further in debt, but we are decreasing the old debt all the time and if we can only sell something (which we are all the time trying to do) we will again be square with the world. At any rate, your father is not worrying about that part of it.[2]

Seattle's early lack of sophistication in terms of its entertainments had by 1914 given way to a growing demand to be up-to-date and to have the latest films and vaudeville. Local theatrical show-men were concerned with pleasing the public, with bringing to the stage entertainment to satisfy the extremes of taste, education, and culture and of course, making money doing it. Initially, the novelty of vaudeville or motion pictures was enough to bring crowds into the theatres. The unadorned

---

2. Stimson/Bullitt correspondence, Dorothy Stimson Bullitt Archives.

nickelodeons set up in downtown Seattle storefronts were thriving businesses from the time they made their first appearance in 1894.

But when the novelty wore thin and competition for paying customers intensified, showmen started to cater to the comforts of customers in a way unheard of except in royal households. Because money was so freely poured into them to please public taste, and because of the freedom designers were given to create imaginative forms, theatre buildings became the temples of the twentieth-century American city. The stage performance in fact often took second billing to the grandeur and exoticism of the auditorium. Three Seattle architects—E.W. Houghton, B. Marcus Priteca, and R.C. Reamer—built regional and national reputations on the basis of their local designs. Two of these architects—Priteca and Reamer—found work with C.D. Stimson that solidified their reputations in the commercial and theatre world.

E. W. Houghton, designer of the Grand Opera House, the first Coliseum Theatre (demolished), and the Moore Theatre was in great demand to design vaudeville and film houses throughout the western states. B. Marcus Priteca had worked for E. W. Houghton until, at age 21, he was hired by Alexander Pantages. Of all Seattle's theatre magnates, its favorite son was Greek-born Alexander Pantages (1876-1936). In 1902, he had arrived in Seattle and opened the Crystal on Second Avenue, where he was manager, ticket taker, janitor, and projectionist.[3]

Soon he was operating the 700-seat Pantages Vaudeville on Second Avenue and Seneca Street and, across the street, the Lois, a 1200-seat house named for his wife. He hired Priteca to design the San Francisco Pantages, located on Market Street. Its opening in 1911 marked the beginning of a long and successful partnership. Their classic Greek facades became the symbol of the Greek theatre magnate. The Oakland Pantages followed. By 1912, he had entered the Canadian market, with theatres in Edmonton and Calgary, to be followed rapidly by built or leasing theatres in Winnipeg, Victoria, and Vancouver. His 1900-seat Seattle Pantages at Third Avenue and University Street became the flagship of the chain in 1915.

Priteca appears to have been a freelancer until 1914, hired on for each job, doing the design work, and then working with local firms to prepare the working drawings and construction documents for Pantages' theatres. Through his association with C. D. Stimson, he was able to establish his own firm, outfit an oak-panelled office in the Seattle Pantages building, and carry on a successful practice as a theatre architect[4]

Architect E.W. Houghton's Moore Theatre of 1907 prior to removal of the side boxes. MOHAI

---

3. Theatre history and biographical information is excerpted from Lawrence Kreisman, "Another Opening, Another Show," *Madison Park Post*, October, 1981.

Crystal Pool advertised "warm ocean water swimming" at Second Avenue and Lenora Street, 1916 SMC.

Priteca's design called for exuberant polychrome terra cotta ornamentation that borrowed from the Italian Renaissance. Mermaids and dolphins tied the facade to the activity within. GG

As the story has been passed down from Stimson to his daughter and granddaughter, C.D. was looking to build a theatre. Priteca turned up for the job and enthusiastically represented his abilities. "I can build a theatre. I know how to build a theatre." And certainly during the preceding years, his experience with Pantages had proved that. Stimson was so taken by his initiative, enterprise, and self-confidence, he thought, "I bet he can do it." But he also knew that he needed start-up money. Priteca told him a long time later he didn't even own a ruler at the time. So Stimson "staked him" to help his starting out costs.[5]

The architectural design for the theatre may have been worked through by Priteca in another project he was asked to undertake at about the same time—design of a "natatorium" (called the Crystal Pool) to be located on property Stimson owned between Second and First avenues and between Virginia and Leonora streets. There was an indoor swimming pool in the Moore Hotel on Second and Virginia Street, and an open-air pool was located at Luna Park in West Seattle. But the Crystal, because of its size and its convenient location, became one of the most popular spots in the city during the

4. In 1912, Priteca designed the Romanesque basilica Temple Bikur Cholim at 17th Avenue and Yesler Way. His most famous local theatre designs were for the Coliseum, the Orpheum at Westlake, and the Pantages at Third and University Street. He was also the consulting architect for the Paramount Theatre at 9th Avenue and Pine Street. In addition to thirty theatres for Pantages, Priteca worked for three other theatre chains, Warner Brothers, the Orpheum Circuit, and Sterling Theatres. From 1940 on, he designed the Admiral, the Magnolia, and remodelled the old civic auditorium into the Seattle Opera House prior to the 1962 Seattle World's Fair.

5. Interview with Priscilla Collins, November 10, 1990.

Crystal Pool interior, 1916. SMC

ensuing decades.[6] Priteca chose a richly ornamented Italian Renaissance terra cotta facade in white with green accents for this building. Green dolphins were the most obvious indication of the purpose of the building. The main entrance to the pavilion was at the corner, a curving vestibule with an ironwork and glass marquee. The bases of two flagpoles were originally designed to incorporate sculptural groups of standing figures in Norse boats, their prows jutting out over the marquees. This part of the design was much simplified in execution. The corner entry was dominated

6. During the 1920s and 1930s, it was the city's most popular indoor pool, and also the scene of Tuesday night boxing cards and prize fights. It was used briefly as a roller skating rink before it was purchased in 1943 by Bethel Temple, Inc., and remodelled as a church. In the process, it lost the prominent corner entrance dome.

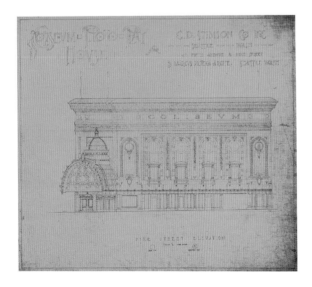

by a great dome, its cupola supporting a full-size statue of Neptune. The interior was impressive, the swimming pool spanned by enormous arched steel trusses supporting a glass roof. Surrounding the pool on three sides were tiers of seats for as many as 1,500 spectators. The pool had salt water piped direct from Elliott Bay, heated, filtered, and chlorinated. A June 30, 1916 caption entitled "Seattle's Latest Bathing Resort," says of it:

> Seattle, with the opening of the Crystal Pool Wednesday night, now has one of the finest natatoriums on the Pacific Coast. The opening of the big swimming pavilion was a brilliant event, combining a program of aquatic events with an elaborate fashion show. Although the seating capacity of the natatorium galleries exceeds 1,500, there were hundreds unable to obtain seats...[7]

The 1,952 seat-Coliseum opened on Jan. 8, 1916, as the first true "motion picture palace." While this was not entirely true—the

---

7. "Seattle's Latest Bathing Resort," *Seattle Times*, June 30, 1916.

Liberty and Colonial Theatres in downtown had also been designed exclusively for film—local advertisements proclaimed it "The World's Largest and Finest Photoplay Palace," and certainly, for a time it was the costliest and most elaborately decorated motion picture theatre—if not in the world, as some claimed, at least west of the major population centers in New York and Chicago. Thousands of curious theatregoers bought tickets ranging from 15 cents to 50 cents for the privilege of viewing the exotic interior and the theatre's first film, "The Cheat," starring Fannie Ward, accompanied by the music of an eight-piece Russian orchestra.

The gleaming, white-glazed terra cotta facades on Fifth Avenue and on Pike Street were Italian Renaissance in style, with urns, garlands, and sacrificial animals displayed in bold relief. All the terra cotta had been manufactured locally, at the Auburn plant of Northern Clay Co. (later to become Gladding, McBean and Company). All of the Italianate details were carefully studied and drawn full size by the architect and then handed over to artisans to construct molds for the many pieces.

Its most impressive feature was the great glass dome and coffered vestibule at the corner of Fifth Avenue and Pike Street, which show a far greater skill in integration with the rest of the facade than did the Crystal Pool entrance. Both corner treatments prefigured Priteca's Los Angeles Pantages Theatre design. The dome acted as a magnet to draw people to the ticket booth; it and the generous ornamental ironwork and glass marquees that extended the length of the theatre were welcoming shelters during the rainy season—for window shoppers at the six retail outlets as well as for ticket holders.[8]

The Roman exterior could only hint at the eclectic fantasies awaiting moviegoers inside the theatre. They entered an Egyptian-inspired lobby decorated in bright Byzantine orange offset with

8. In 1950, Priteca was in charge of a $250,000 remodel in which the domed entrance was replaced with a cylindrical neon tribute to Hollywood topped with a life-sized revolving golden Oscar. A threatened lawsuit by the Academy of Motion Picture Arts for use of the trademark resulted in the removal of Oscar from its pedestal.

The theatre was managed by a succession of companies: Jensen and Von Herberg; Fox West Coast; Evergreen; and Luxury Theatres. In April, 1967, the Bullitt Company sold it to Broadacres, Inc., a real estate firm headed by one of its original investors, Joe Gottstein. At this writing the theatre is closed and awaiting adaptive reuse to retail.

Above, Coliseum Theatre procenium arch and Egyptian mosaic dome, 1916. MOHAI

The Mother Goose muraled nursery in the Coliseum Theatre, 1916. MOHAI

black, pale greens, and dull reds. The lotus flower, a sacred symbol of regeneration and fertility to the Egyptians, was used thematically here and in the theatre auditorium. Oval domes overhead were surrounded by painted allegorical figures of Cleopatra's Egypt. Mosaic carpeting was set off by soft gray and black furnishings and sculptured wall designs. But the exoticism of the theatre was far-reaching. There was a Turkish men's smoking room, a Japanese-styled lounge for the ladies, and a children's nursery with Mother Goose figures and ducks decorating the walls.

The theatre had one balcony and an innovation of Priteca's to theatre design—a mezzanine level designed to fill the acoustic dead space formed by the balcony. Both were reached by ramps, stairs and an elevator with a 27 person capacity—reputed to be the first elevator in a picture house.

The auditorium combined both Classical and Egyptian decorative motifs with some flair. There were excellent sight lines and indirect lighting that accented the decorative elements and avoided glare. Originally, organ pipes decorated the side of the proscenium, two electric fountains illuminated either side of the orchestra pit, and thirty canaries sang in the upstairs foyer. The valance of the giant stage curtains featured embroidered lotus flowers from the Nile, and Cleopatra posed in a painted medallion above the stage. Plaster grotesques and classical mouldings appeared throughout the auditorium, particularly in the steeply graded balcony. And if the movie was less than absorbing, the patrons could always look up at a display of the evening heavens, the Big Dipper and North Star sparkling electrically over the balcony.

Above, A comedic grotesque smiles down at theatre-goers from its perch. GG

Above right, Egyptian motif colored mosaic tile with asps in the theatre lobby. MOHAI

The south facade of the Coliseum Theatre. GG

THE MILLION DOLLAR THEATRE

The success of the Coliseum Theatre in 1916 did not go unnoticed by Stimson. He saw the growing opportunities in the entertainment industry and looked to his other real estate holdings for similar developments. He and his brother Frederick and their children had received the Muskegon building at Third Street and Broadway in Los Angeles as part of the estate settlement from their father. In the first decades of the twentieth century, this Broadway was emerging as a sister to New York's Broadway and the predecessor to Hollywood Boulevard in its many vaudeville and film houses. Investment there would produce some of the most glamorous motion picture palaces in the country, beginning with the Million Dollar Theatre of 1917 and culminating in the Los Angeles Theatre of 1931. And the initiator of the Million Dollar—the trendsetter of the motion picture palace in Los Angeles, was none other than C.D. Stimson.

Entrance and marquee, Million Dollar Theatre, 1918. LAPL

Million Dollar Theatre and Edison Building. LAPL

Million Dollar Theatre auditorium and procenium arch. LAPL

It is unclear whether C.D. and Frederick took the initiative or were approached by a consortium of Los Angeles businessmen known as the Stability Building Company with the concept. In any case, the Stimsons chose to offer the group a ninety-nine year lease on the property for the purpose of building the new Broadway skyscraper. Homer Laughlin, president of the company, happened to be the owner of the Grand Central Market building next door. Ironically, the Citizens' Trust and Savings Bank, which acted as treasurer of the company, was the bank headed by Thomas D. Stimson two decades earlier.

The Edison Building, as it came to be known, was thirteen stories tall—the maximum height allowed under the city's restrictive earthquake code. The upper floors were planned to house studios and lofts "intended to meet the special requirements of the film concerns centering in this, the capital of moviedom." The major tenant actually became the Southern California Edison Company which, after merging with Pacific Light and Power in 1917, needed a large headquarters downtown.[9]

The building was designed by Albert C. Martin Sr. William L. Woolett designed the theatre proper for D. J. Grauman and his son Sid Grauman—his first such venture, to be followed by the Egyptian and Chinese theatres in Hollywood. The design for the Edison Building and its Million Dollar was anything but restrained. The Nov. 26, 1916, Real Estate and Development Section of the *Los Angeles Sunday Times* put it aptly in the headline, "Splendid Spanish Renaissance Pile for Broadway at Third: City's most imposing building is started."

It borrowed heavily from the Spanish Churrigueresque in its facade ornamentation—perhaps because the style had gained so much popularity in 1915 at both the Panama-Pacific Expositions in San Diego and San Francisco, and because southern California designers embraced the Spanish Colonial mission style so frequently in its homes, tourist facilities, and commercial buildings.

But the Spanish-derived ornament was only a part of the theatre's fantastic array of decorative devices. It was also very much an American institution, its facade sculptures and bas reliefs filled with popular western imagery. There were longhorn cattle skulls, resplendent with life-size bronze horns sharing space with volutes and ornate mouldings; bison head corbels supported a silent-screen

9. Million Dollar Theatre and Edison Building clipping file, Los Angeles Conservancy offices.

parade of statues representing the Fine Arts, including an exotic Balinese maiden symbolizing Dance, a gentleman with a smock and palette for Painting, and of course, a cinematographer behind his Camera.[10]

As *The LA Sunday Times* described it,

> The architect, Albert C. Martin, was asked at the beginning by the projectors to design a building that, while reflecting the sentiment of Southern Californians with regard to Spanish types, should at the same time breathe the spirit of the modern theatre...In the florid style of the Spanish renaissance there will be wrought bas reliefs, decorative panels, and figures in repose and action depicting the motion picture industry and other phases of present day thought and activity instead of the quaint medieval details ordinarily dug up and slavishly copied from European prototypes.

The lobby, finished in bronze, marble, and stucco made to look like gilded and colored woodwork, featured ceiling and wall murals and rich arabesque decoration. The theatre interior was hexagonal in plan and 60-feet-high topped by a flat oval dome featuring a 25- foot mural painting with heroic winged figures of tragedy and comedy surrounded by dancing forms. Two huge white Corinthian columns flanked the stage, and a great mural over the proscenium depicted a winged figure representing the spirit of the future.

Because of the shortage of steel during 1917, the structural design of the theatre had to be redefined using "the world's longest concrete arch" to support the weight of the balcony instead of the planned steel truss. The local papers were fascinated when the arch supported ten times the expected weight of the gallery—1.5 million pounds—to satisfy building department inspectors as to the safety of this unique solution.

When the theatre opened with the premiere of William S. Hart's "The Silent Man" on Feb. 1, 1918, a crowd two blocks long cheered the arrival of Charlie Chaplin, Mary Pickford, the Gish sisters, Douglas Fairbanks, William S. Hart, D.W. Griffith, Mack Sennett, and Cecil B. de Mille.[11]

10. Charles Moore, Peter Becker, Regula Campbell, *The City Observed: Los Angeles* (New York: Vintage Books,1984), 26.

11. The Graumans gave up interest in the theatre in the late 1920s. Fox West Coast took over through the 1940s, when it was leased by a Latin American entrepreneur, Frank Fouce. It has shown Spanish language films with occasional stage shows to the present. The original 3,500 seat capacity has been reduced to 2,350. There are currently plans to renovate the theatre and the adjoining Public Market.

The flamboyant Spanish Churrigueresque ornamentation is combined with western American imagery in the form of longhorn cattle skulls that frame the arch. LK

One of a series of buffalo head corbels support a cornice. One of the sculptural forms is an actor holding the masks of comedy and tragedy. LK

METROPOLITAN CENTER

Above, Stimson Mill company in Ballard, ca. 1910. DSB

Stimson Mill Company office in Ballard, designed by K.K. Cutter, has undergone a number of alterations during 90 years of use. GG

    C.D. Stimson's last years in Seattle are strikingly parallel to those of his father forty years earlier in Los Angeles. They are a record of commitments to downtown that included his own building projects, his financial support of other civic projects, and his generously given time and energy to various boards and commissions. It was through these involvements that he and his son Thomas made the acquaintance of R. C. Reamer, an architect who would have an important role in designing commercial projects for the Stimsons in the late 1920s.[12]

    Stimson was an influential member of the board of the Metropolitan Building Company, founded in 1907 to develop the University Tract lands. The board consisted of eleven members, each of whom had distinguished himself in Seattle commerce and industry. One of these founding members, Mr. George W. Emerson,

12. In addition to his work associated with the Stimson family, Reamer's reputation in the Pacific Northwest is based on his Great Northern Building and Seattle Times Building in Seattle, which combined classicism and Art Deco modernism, and the Art Deco Fox Theatre in Spokane. His most innovative design was the Edmond Meany Hotel (1931) an exposed concrete and glass highrise that bridged the gap between Art Deco and International styled modernism.

described the conditions of the site and the mission of the company in these words:

> It is seldom given to any body of city builders to act as a unit in the building of the very center of a large city; seldom that a tract of many acres can be found, unimproved, with the retail district of a city of two hundred thousand people bounding it on two sides, and the better portion of the resident district abutting upon the other two sides; a tract comparatively level, with paved and finished streets to the east, west, north and south; where the grading and widening have been done or soon will be, where all things are ready for that extension and for permanent buildings for which tenants wait.
>
> In the very heart of such a city, we are called upon to grade and pave our streets and build acres of commercial blocks—to build a city within a city. No grander task has fallen to any body of men, no grander chance to accomplish great results with few mistakes. Symmetry, beauty, adaptability and economy in construction should be easy to attain under these conditions and the city that we build should be a marvel among the cities of the world.[13]

Stimson brought to the company his experience in real estate development and business management. He became a stockholder shortly after the formation of the company and, as offerings were made for the buildings to be constructed in the development, he and his family members increased their holdings until they became the largest owners in the company. By 1926, the C.D. Stimson Company held a quarter interest, more than twice as much as any other single stockholder in the organization. His involvement was reflected in his role on the board. Elected to the board of trustees at the annual meeting in 1916, he became vice president in 1922 and president in 1925. He also assumed directorship of the Metropolitan National Bank at the Center in 1917 and was an organizer and director of the General Insurance Company of America (now known as Safeco).

The earliest buildings, the Cobb Medical Center and the White, Henry and Stuart blocks, followed the designs of the New York firm of John Mead Howells and I.N. Phelps Stokes with A.H. Albertson as associate. The buildings were of similar height (11 stories) and materials (brick and terra cotta) in a dignified Beaux Arts style. These and all subsequent buildings provided retail on the ground floors. The Metropolitan Theatre of 1911 deviated from the original plan, as did the Arena in 1915 and Cobb Building

C.D. Stimson's 9th floor corner office in the White Building, ca. 1910.

13. *The Metropolitan Bulletin*, 8, No. 15, (Dec. 21, 1923), 6.

Metropolitan Center: University Street with Cobb Building (left) open and White Henry and Stuart Building almost complete. SMC

Annex in 1921. In January, 1923, the group of office buildings and shops which were variously called "University Tract" and "Metropolitan Building Company" were officially christened "Metropolitan Center."

Stimson and other businessmen banded together in 1922 to support a community hotel. C.D. was appointed chair of the planning committee and reviewed a number of proposals from local property owners before selecting the site recommended by the Metropolitan Building Company. The Chamber of Commerce took charge of financing the $5 million building of the hotel. C.D. was elected vice-president of the Community Hotel Corporation Board of Trustees. When a shortage of funds threatened to compromise the design of the building, C.D. stepped in to purchase additional

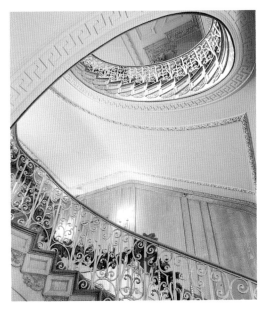

stocks and bonds in the company, making him the largest single owner in the corporation. His investment resulted in the completion in 1924 of Seattle's grande dame of hotels, the Olympic, a brick and terra cotta faced Italian palazzo designed by the prestigious New York firm of George Post. The hotel name was, in fact, Stimson's preference, an homage to his favorite yacht, *Olympic*.

The Stimson Building designed by Howells and Albertson was named for C.D. by an appreciative board of directors toward their president. It became the second structure in the University Tract built exclusively for the use of physicians and dentists. Stimson had suggested that use. Its modified-Georgian, brick and terra cotta facade extended the length of Fourth Avenue between University and Seneca Streets. A two-story barrel-vaulted-and-coffered en-

Above left, The White Henry Stuart Building, corner of Fourth Avenue and Union Street. SMC

Above right, Cobb Building, detail of the cornice with Chief Seattle busts. GG

Below left, The Olympic Hotel spiral staircase sports its Christmas finery. GG.

Below right, Olympic Hotel from Seneca Street and Fourth Avenue, 1929. SMC

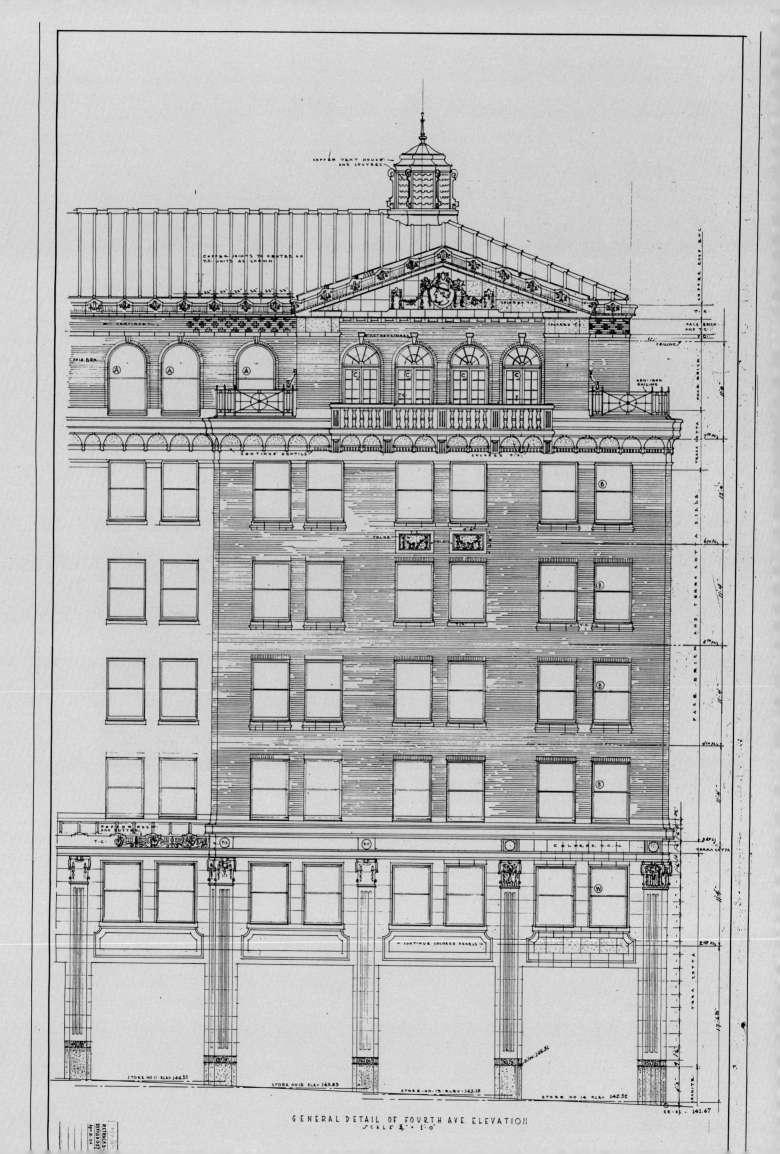

GENERAL DETAIL OF FOURTH AVE. ELEVATION
SCALE ¼" = 1'-0"

trance lobby panelled and paved with Sienna gray and Tennessee pink marble greeted its users. There were setbacks on the seventh floor that provided terraces for these offices. The top floor also featured semicircular headed windows and balustrades. Two prominent terra cotta pediments with bas reliefs of Asclepius, God of Healing, dominated the north and south wings of the building. According to a Metropolitan Bulletin description, "Of heroic proportions, befitting the god to whom the Greeks erected at Epidaurus one of the most famous of temples, the great bas-reliefs fill the decorative spaces in the pediments at either end of the building. The head, done in buff terra cotta, is silhouetted against an oval background of sage green terra cotta."[14]

In the midst of these downtown projects, Stimson encouraged and promoted the establishment of Seattle's Fifth Avenue entertainment district—a district not unlike the Broadway District in Los Angeles that his Million Dollar Theatre had inspired. The Coliseum Theatre had started it in 1916; the opening of the Fifth Avenue Theatre by the Metropolitan Building Company in 1926

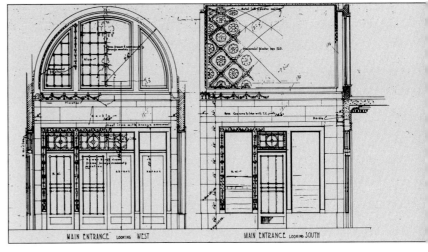

MAIN ENTRANCE LOOKING WEST   MAIN ENTRANCE LOOKING SOUTH

Far left, Elevation of one corner of the medical building designed by Howells and Albertson that would be named for C.D. Stimson. UW

Stimson Building shortly after completion. DSB

Main entrance and ceiling details, Stimson Building. UW

14. *The Metropolitan Bulletin*, 8, No. 27, (Oct. 10, 1924), 7.

**Skinner Building and Fifth Avenue
Theatre on opening night,
September 1926. MOHAI**

and the opening of John Hamrick's Music Box Theatre midway
between the two in 1928 completed a district that stretched from the
Metropolitan Theatre on University Street north to the glamorous
Orpheum Theatre at Westlake.

Harry C. Arthur, Jr. had been General Manager of West
Coast Theatres, Inc., the largest intra-state theatre circuit in the
world, when he took over as President of Pacific Northwest Theatres, then the largest circuit of theatres in the Pacific Northwest. By
1926, the corporation had absorbed the Jensen and Von Herberg
chain of over 40 theatres (including Stimson's Coliseum) and was
rapidly adding new theatres, to include the Fifth Avenue in Seattle,
the Broadway in Portland, and the Mt. Baker in Bellingham. The
Stimsons became the largest local subscribers to the debentures and
common stock of the company; Thomas D. Stimson was one of
three vice-presidents and he and his father C.D. sat on the board of
directors.

Architect R.C. Reamer had been hired by the Metropolitan
Building Company to design what would become the Olympic

Hotel. The United Hotel Corporation, which was slated to operate the hotel, refused to sign the lease unless its company architects, George Post of New York, drew the plans. Reamer lost the commission, but the Metropolitan hired him as house architect, a position that provided him with important commissions downtown. His first major work was the Skinner Building of 1925-26 along Fifth Avenue between Union and University streets. It represented a successful adaptation of the Italian Renaissance to an office block. The subtle, dignified character of the sandstone-faced building, with its mock loggia and tile roofing, belied the exotic and extraordinarily colorful interior of the Fifth Avenue Theatre within—the largest and the most authentic example of traditional Chinese timber architecture and decoration outside of Asia.[15]

They spent $1.5 million to evoke the Temple of Heavenly Peace in the Forbidden City and a Ming dynasty royal audience hall dominated by a great dome. The one difference—and it was significant—was that all of the rounded posts, stenciled beams, layered brackets, dragons, birds and flowers were made of plaster, cleverly disguised to pass as wood. It was largely through the knowledge and skills of Gustav Liljestrom, chief designer at S. and J. Gump in San Francisco and an expert in Chinese decoration, that the project succeeded so well.

The opening night program educated theatregoers to the splendors around and above them:

Lobby of Fifth Avenue Theatre festooned, possibly for Christmas festivities, 1926. MOHAI

Entrance vestibule on Fifth Avenue, showing doors with gold good luck knobs. MOHAI

---

15. Lawrence Kreisman, "Weaver of Dreams," *Pacific*, Seattle Times Magazine, Jan. 8, 1989, 16.

Perhaps its most imposing feature is the great dome, as elsewhere throughout the theatre, its symbolic themes borrowed from Chinese legends, it motifs from Chinese poetry. Coiled within an azure sphere and surrounded by glowing hues of cloud-red, emblematic of calamity and warfare; blue, of rain; green symbolic of plague; black, of floods; and gold, of prosperity—is the Great Dragon, guardian of the heavens and foe of evil spirits. He is, indeed, the brooding genius of the place, his presence shadowed and multiplied in varying shapes and forms throughout the structure.[16]

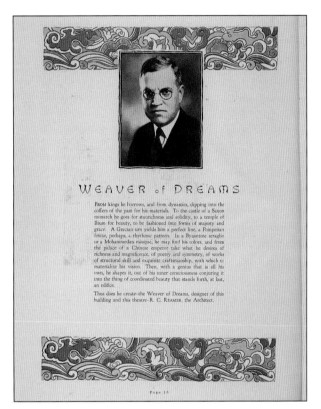

WEAVER of DREAMS

FROM kings he borrows, and from dynasties, dipping into the coffers of the past for his materials. To the castle of a Saxon monarch he goes for staunchness and solidity, to a temple of Ilium for beauty, to be fashioned into forms of majesty and grace. A Grecian urn yields him a perfect line, a Pompeiian frieze, perhaps, a rhythmic pattern. In a Byzantine seraglio or a Mohammedan mosque, he may find his colors, and from the palace of a Chinese emperor take what he desires of richness and magnificence, of poetry and symmetry, of works of structural skill and exquisite craftsmanship, with which to materialize his vision. Then, with a genius that is all his own, he shapes it, out of his inner consciousness conjuring it into the thing of coordinated beauty that stands forth, at last, an edifice.

Thus does he create–the Weaver of Dreams, designer of this building and this theatre–R. C. REAMER, the Architect.

Robert C. Reamer, Weaver of Dreams, from Opening night program, Fifth Avenue Theatre, 1926.

Poetry and legend were not only the province of the architecture but of the architect as well. In a misty, romantic homage to R.C. Reamer, the program painted him in almost God-like terms as "Weaver of Dreams." The view presented was that architects, endowed with creative genius and trained to recognize and interpret the architecture and decorative styles of every culture, could pick and choose among them to come up with the perfect building.

From kings he borrows, and from dynasties, dipping into the coffers of the past for his materials. To the castle of a Saxon monarch he goes for staunchness and solidity, to a temple of Ilium for beauty, to be fashioned into forms of majesty and grace. A Grecian urn yields him a perfect line, a Pompeiian frieze, perhaps, a rhythmic pattern. In a Byzantine seraglio or a Mohammedan mosque, he may find his colors, and from the palace of a Chinese emperor take what he desires of richness and magnificence, of poetry and symmetry, of works of structural skill and exquisite craftsmanship, with which to materialize his vision. Then, with a genius that is all his own, he shapes it, out of his inner consciousnessconjuring it into the thing of coordinated beauty that stands forth, at last, an edifice. Thus does he create—the Weaver of Dreams, designer of this building and this theatre--R.C. Reamer, the Architect.[17]

---

16. Fifth Avenue Theatre opening night program, (dress rehearsal copy dated September 23, 1926), private collection, 5.

17. Fifth Avenue Theatre program, 10.

Auditorium, Fifth Avenue Theatre.
Dick Busher (DB)

The theatre's opening was a major event, drawing crowds comparable to the population that gathered on Armistice Night, 1918, in the downtown streets. Those fortunate enough to attend the performance would have enjoyed a variety of cinema, live music, and stage shows. The program featured guest organist Oliver Wallace on the ascending Wurlitzer: a filmed travelogue; Lipschultz and his syncopating soloists in a musicale, appropriately entitled "Orientale"; a scenic poem filmed by Robert Bruce; the Fanchon and Marco stage show featuring Boyce Combe and the Sunkist Beauty Revue; and the feature film that night, Cecil B. DeMille's "Young April."

With the Million Dollar, the Coliseum, and the Fifth Avenue drawing thousands of patrons, Stimson was quick to recognize the financial advantages of motion picture theatres. In August, 1923, he had purchased lots on Fifth Avenue in the block south of his Coliseum Theatre. Grote Rankin Company was located at the north corner, and Stimson purchased from that family The Sun Building, a two-story terra cotta-faced retail and office building, and an adjoining mid-block lot then occupied by a three-story brick rooming house built in 1904. He leased the latter to John Hemrick, local theatre entrepreneur, for the purpose of building a movie theatre, the Music Box. Hamrick had already built several silent motion picture houses, the Colonial Theatre at 1515 Fourth Avenue in 1913, and The Blue Mouse, across the street from Stimson's Fifth Avenue property, in 1920.

Completed and opened in 1928, the Music Box Theatre was reported to be the first in Seattle designed exclusively for sound motion pictures or "talkies." Hamrick had witnessed the tryout of the Vitaphone sound system invented by Bell Laboratories while visiting New York City in 1926. He had installed it in the Blue Mouse in 1927 and, confident that it was the next great step in the evolution of motion pictures, had his new theatre specially designed to accommodate Vitaphone and Movie tone systems.[18]

The Music Box was designed by the Seattle firm of Henry Bittman in a restrained, Spanish Renaissance style. Bittman's firm had prepared plans for a number of important downtown buildings, including the Eagles Auditorium, the Decatur Building, the Equitable Savings Bank, and the Mann Building and Embassy Theatre. Bittman took responsibility for attracting clients and for the structural aspects of projects while Harold Adams, his chief designer, worked on his most important commissions.

The beige brick facade of the Music Box was dominated by three tall cast-stone-sculpted window surrounds. The cast stone cornice incorporated two alternating shield ornaments and finial and scallop ornamental crests. The auditorium, which seated over 700 people, had side walls with recessed panels bordered by gilt-turned pilasters and ceiling "beams" (plasterwork treated to look like timber) with richly stenciled geometric ornament in the dominant colors of green, gold, and black with additional accents. Amber glass chandeliers hung from ornate plaster bases fixed to the ceiling. The proscenium arch was heavily modeled and featured a running pattern of arches, with heraldic shield ornaments in niches comparable to the ornament on the exterior cornice. The theatre's

Grote Rankin Co., Sun Building, and Music Box Theatre, c. 1925. SMC

18. Landmark Nomination Form submitted by Ellen Miller-Wolfe, Donald Andrew Kunz, December 28, 1984, Office of Urban Conservation, City of Seattle.

style may have influenced Sherwood Ford's design of the much larger Mayflower Theatre (also known as the Music Hall) at Seventh Avenue and Olive Way and his original design for the facade of the Washington Athletic Club, both done in 1929. Ford had reputedly been the designer for the Embassy Theatre and the two men would therefore have worked together.

A METROPOLITAN CENTER IN BELLINGHAM

It was clear from the experience of the Metropolitan Building Company with its Olympic Hotel, Fifth Avenue Theatre, and office blocks, that well-planned hotels, theatres, and commercial structures in close proximity brought glamor and excitement to the streets of Seattle while bolstering the local economy. Quick to respond to this trend, the C.D. Stimson Company formed the Bellingham Development Company and purchased land near the commercial heart of Bellingham, Washington, another city whose economy was largely based in lumber. The intent was to replicate, on a smaller scale, the successes of the Seattle venture. Thomas D. Stimson was elected president; Major J. F. Douglas, manager of the Metropolitan Building Company was made director; Walter T. Douglas took the role of secretary and assistant manager; George S. Douglas was named manager of the company. He was also named directing manager of the theatre, with Harry C. Arthur Jr. as operator and R. C. Reamer the natural choice to design the new buildings. They moved incredibly quickly, making their initial visit to Bellingham on Feb. 27, 1926 and completing purchase of the property on North Commercial Street by mid-March for $200,000. Ground was broken for the theatre April 6th. The two-story Reveille Harold block, facing Commercial and Champion streets, was also remodelled and became known as the Douglas Building. Fourteen months later, on Apr. 29, 1927, the theatre opened its doors to 5,000 people.[19]

For the Mt. Baker Theatre, Reamer tapped the reliable sources he had already established for the Skinner Building and Fifth Avenue Theatre, then well under construction. He ordered Wilkeson sandstone to face the building and the identical seating as at the Fifth. From most of the same suppliers, he bought marble, tile, stone, furnishings, and the Wurlitzer organ. Unlike the Fifth Avenue, which was encircled by an office block, the Mt. Baker Theatre

Thomas Douglas Stimson, ca. 1925. SMC

---

19. Information about the Mt. Baker Theatre comes from Dorothy Koert, *A History of Whatcom County Theatre* (Lyndon, Washington: *Lyndon Tribune*, 1979), 65-71.

building was to be freestanding. A single story of retail shops would front the theatre on two sides. Consequently, the Spanish style could spill over to the exterior in the form of tile roofs and an octagonal tower of stucco over steel rising 110 feet high. This minaret culminated in an arched dome surmounted by a large, revolving searchlight that had been aboard the battleship Oregon when it rounded Cape Horn in 1898 during the Spanish-American war.

Reamer adapted the Spanish Renaissance style for the interiors--already well-represented elsewhere in American motion picture palaces. The foyer was described as evoking "the mellow atmosphere of Old Spain." Its mottled, buff plaster walls, grand stairways, columned arcades, sloped ceilings of grained-wood paneling and beams hand-decorated in colorful Spanish designs "have the softened hues of antiquity as though time had dusted them with tender hand." In the auditorium, massive beams were stenciled in red and gold to create the

illusion of wood inlay, and elaborate cornice and side-wall arched ornaments were created in plaster and richly colored in orange, blue, buff, and gold. The great dome, eighty feet in diameter, was said to gather into a glowing cluster all the rich color and shimmering gold of walls and ceiling and present it "in a bouquet of massive ornamental forms." From the dome hung a six-hundred-pound chandelier of antique bronze. The stage was then the largest in the state at 80 x 30 feet, and the company installed the latest in lighting and projection equipment.

  Across the street from the Mt. Baker Theatre, the Bellingham Development Company erected a new hotel building that, at 15 stories, overshadowed the traditional building heights of the small city. Initially, Reamer designed a three-tiered, set-back skyscraper and chose to clothe the facade in a Spanish Renaissance style that would complement the theatre. The two-story base of the building extending to fill the property line would encompass ground floor retail and entrances. The second floor would house the public functions of the hotel, including the ballrooms and meeting rooms. A rich, terra cotta cornice would crown this base. Above this was to be a two-story setback block with a rich cornice and balustrade that would form the base for a ten-story tower. The tower in turn would be crowned by a penthouse floor detailed with tapestry brick and with champhered corners opening up to terraces. The whole composition would be richly laid out with ornamental terra cotta evocative of the Spanish Baroque.

  The building, as built, was a much more modest effort in the up-to-date "modernistic" style being favored in office construction in New York, Chicago, and, by 1927—with the construction of the Northern Life Tower under way—in Seattle as well. The elaborate cornices, full of scrollwork, urns, finials, and balusters, were eliminated and replaced by simple banding. The two-story setback tower base was scaled back to two sides rather than all four. The penthouse floor was set back with vertical piers leading the eye upward to a steel tower nearly as tall as the building itself on which the illuminated name Bellingham Hotel could be seen for miles. Instead of the rich, applied ornamentation derived from the Renaissance tradition, the building's ornament was restrained, low bas relief placed in the spandrel sections where they did not interrupt the clean, upward sweep of the vertical piers. The ornamental vocabulary was new—fresh from the Exposition of Decorative and Industrial Arts held in Paris in 1925.

Far left, The concrete shell of the Mt. Baker Theatre takes shape. Galen Biery Collection (GB)

Far Left, The richly detailed foyer of the theatre. Double stairways lead to a columned promenade. GB

Above, The completed theatre awaits opening night and tenants for its retail spaces. GB

Below, Mt. Baker Theatre, 1988. LK

The two building designs reflect Reamer's willingness to embrace new thinking. The work that came from his firm between 1926 and 1931 was influenced by traditional, classically based design and the new modernistic styles. In his travels, Reamer had been touched by the spirit of the "new architecture" in New York, Chicago, and Los Angeles. His firm experimented with the new decorative vocabulary in the Great Northern Building and the 1411 Fourth Avenue Building at the same time as they worked on the

Far left, Rendering of Bellingham Hotel in the Spanish Renaissance style. DSB

Left, Hotel as built ca. 1930. DSB

Bellingham Hotel. These 1928 buildings had clean, box-like forms, incised decorative panels, chevron and fern-filled friezes, and set-back parapets. They offered a compromised modernism— up-to-date without being radical.[20]

1411 FOURTH AVENUE

Stimson initiated a division of his many properties and investment stocks into two separate entities in 1927-the C.D. Stimson Company and the Stimson Realty Company. The estate was a complicated one; he saw the importance of providing equally for his two children, Thomas and Dorothy, and having it all cleanly done with their knowledge before his death. Thomas, as head of the C.D. Stimson Company, would own nearly all of Stimson's real estate holdings with the exception of the two major revenue generators, the Coliseum Theatre and the Fourth and Union Street property (where the 1411 Fourth Avenue Building would rise), and parcels at First Avenue and Pine Street and at Pike Street and Harvard Avenue which were to be Dorothy's. Thomas also would

Elevator lobby, 1411 Fourth Avenue. GG

20. Kreisman, "Weaver of Dreams," *Pacific,* 16

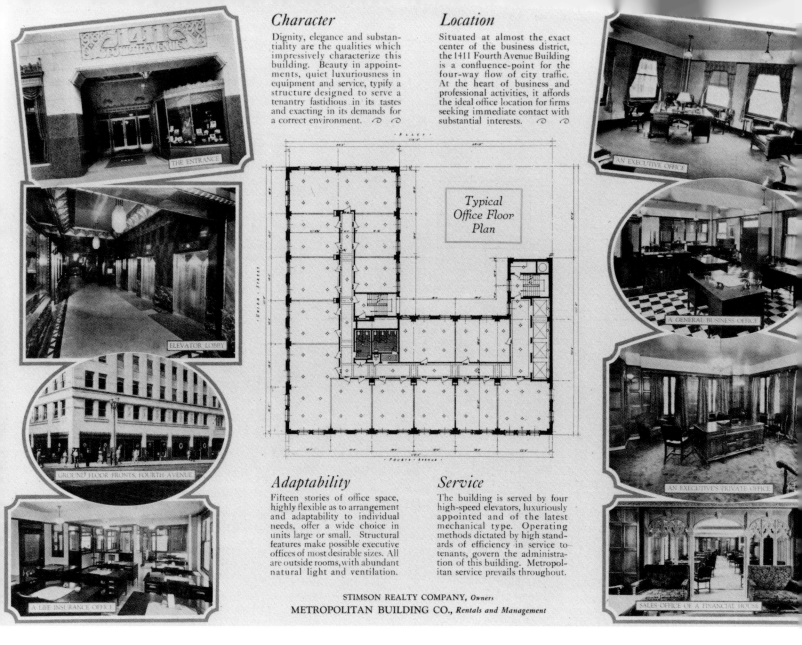

Character

Dignity, elegance and substantiality are the qualities which impressively characterize this building. Beauty in appointments, quiet luxuriousness in equipment and service, typify a structure designed to serve a tenantry fastidious in its tastes and exacting in its demands for a correct environment.

Location

Situated at almost the exact center of the business district, the 1411 Fourth Avenue Building is a confluence-point for the four-way flow of city traffic. At the heart of business and professional activities, it affords the ideal office location for firms seeking immediate contact with substantial interests.

Typical Office Floor Plan

Adaptability

Fifteen stories of office space, highly flexible as to arrangement and adaptability to individual needs, offer a wide choice in units large or small. Structural features make possible executive offices of most desirable sizes. All are outside rooms, with abundant natural light and ventilation.

Service

The building is served by four high-speed elevators, luxuriously appointed and of the latest mechanical type. Operating methods dictated by high standards of efficiency in service to tenants, govern the administration of this building. Metropolitan service prevails throughout.

STIMSON REALTY COMPANY, *Owners*
METROPOLITAN BUILDING CO., *Rentals and Management*

THE ENTRANCE · ELEVATOR LOBBY · GROUND FLOOR FRONTS, FOURTH AVENUE · A LIFE INSURANCE OFFICE · AN EXECUTIVE OFFICE · A GENERAL BUSINESS OFFICE · AN EXECUTIVE'S PRIVATE OFFICE · SALES OFFICE OF A FINANCIAL HOUSE

The Stimson Realty Co. sales brochure . UW

Frosted glass chandelier in the lobby repeats elevator door motifs. GG.

receive the stock in the Metropolitan Building Company; the Olympic Development Company; Rainier National Park; St. Nicholas School; Pacific Northwest Theatres; Wenatchee Development Company; Seattle Tennis Club bonds; the mill, lumber and logging company; and $621,000 in cash. Dorothy, as head of Stimson Realty Company, would control the rest of the properties, along with bonds for the Metropolitan Building Company, stocks and bonds in the Olympic Hotel, Pacific Northwest Theatres, General Insurance Company, and $340,000 in cash.[21]

T.D. Stimson had planned his Douglas Building in Los Angeles as a cornerstone of the commercial district there shortly before his death. Coincidentally, C.D. Stimson's development career culminated, in 1928 in the plans for a major new office building at the northwest corner of Fourth and Union Street designed by architect R.C. Reamer. However C.D. lived to see his plan completed.

Stimson had bought the property from O.O. Denny for $25,000. in November, 1900. A brick building with stores on the

---

21. C.D. Stimson Records, Dorothy Stimson Bullitt Archives

1411 Fourth Avenue ca. 1928 DSB

ground floor and the Antler's Hotel on the upper two floors occupied the site until 1928. The new building was constructed at a cost of $1.1 million. At 15 stories in height, 1411 Fourth Avenue was neither the tallest nor the largest building in the city. But its owner was at least able to say with some assurance that it was the tallest edifice in the city to be built entirely of stone facing, following the examples of Reamer's other buildings nearby, the Wilkeson sandstone-clad Skinner Building (1926) and the limestone-clad Great Northern Building (1928). By contrast, earlier buildings, like the Cobb, White Henry Stuart, Olympic Hotel, and Metropolitan Theatre were clad in brick with terra cotta used extensively at the base and crown.

In planning the building, Stimson had taken the recom-

mendations of his contractor, George Teufel, the mind behind
much of the Metropolitan Building Company construction. On
Feb. 10, 1928, son-in-law Scott Bullitt wrote to the Stimsons at the
Huntington Hotel in Pasadena:

> Teufel said that there would be a difference of about $30,000
> if brick with terra cotta trim should be used instead of stone on the
> 4th Avenue and Union Street fronts. There could also be a saving
> of $12,000 to $15,000 if terrazzo should be used on the floors instead
> of marble. They seemed to think that was not wise economy in the
> long run.

Washington State Architect focused attention on the
architect's choice of materials in a November, 1928 article.

> The lovely soft light gray cut stone exterior of 1411 Fourth
> Avenue lends impressive dignity to the architectural lines and
> weaves soft shadows which seem to deepen the vertical lines and
> give a picture effect, restful and pleasing.

While the shape of the building was essentially box-like,
its recessed spandrels, unadorned vertical piers, and gentle set-
back pillars at the parapet did much to make it appear a skyscraper.

A rendering of the building is featured on a 1937 Christmas card from the staff and management of the Stimson Realty Company. DSB

The 1411 Fourth Avenue Building facades were rich in textural incised-relief panels and ornamental bands derived from Celtic interlacing and bestiary motifs, as well as the more familiar chevron and stylized-floral motifs associated with the contemporary French decorative arts movement later referred to as "Art Deco." The vestibule and lobby areas were richly appointed with Honduran mahogany panelling, cast-bronze elevator doors and mouldings, carved friezes, and sandblasted-and-etched glass chandeliers that were as up-to-date as anything in New York or Chicago.

Because of its location directly across the street from the Great Northern Railway ticket office, the street-level retail shops at 1411 Fourth Avenue quickly became the location for railroad and steamship company sales offices, including the Northern Pacific, Union Pacific, Southern Pacific, Western Pacific, Atchison, Topeka and Santa Fe, and Alaska Steamship Companies, most of which had occupied space on the ground floor of the Antler's Building prior to its demolition for Stimson's new building. These tenants, along with offices of most of the major insurance companies and broker-age houses, made the corner of Fourth and Union Street the city's transportation headquarters and a financial hub.[22]

Bronze trim in the vestibule at 1411 Fourth Avenue. GG

---

22. 1411 Fourth Avenue Building Seattle Landmark Nomination form prepared by Lawrence Kreisman, Office of Urban Conservation, City of Seattle.

The library at Brookwood, the C.W.
Stimson residence. UW

Background, Architect Charles
Platt's rendering of the east
elevation of Thomas and Emma
Stimson residence, 1924. SMC

Chapter 7

ARCHITECTURE IN THE FAMILY ENCLAVE

Harriet Stimson with grandchildren. Left to right: Frances, Nona, David (above), Douglas (baby in lap) Priscilla, and Stimson. DSB

C.D. and Harriet Stimson had built Norcliffe with the expectation that the extended family would be there often, either living with them or visiting for weekends and vacations. Like Thomas Douglas and Achsah before them, they had brought up their children to believe in the importance of family and in the bonds that kept family together. The Highlands bluff south of Norcliffe became, over time, the setting for a family enclave—each home designed or remodelled by a significant local or nationally recognized architect and gardens often attended to by prominent landscape firms. It was as though the tradition of building begun by Thomas Douglas and passed down to his sons had spread its influence to many others.

The most distinguished home to be built was Thomas D. Stimson's, designed by the important New York architect Charles Platt to the specific requirements of Stimson's wife, Emma, whom he married in June, 1914. Emma's father, J. A. Baillargeon was a French Canadian who had come to California around 1850 and worked for the Schwabacher's department store in San Francisco. Eventually, he moved to Seattle and founded Baillargeon's Lace House, specializing in imported dry goods. He had married Anne Collins, one of the daughters of John Collins, lumberman, real estate developer, and mayor of Seattle.[1] Emma was one of five

1. Coincidentally, John Collins' other daughter, Emma, married Archibald Downey, the engineer for the Highlands project, whose *Colindown* stood between the Bullitt and C.W. Stimson estates. Built in 1921 and designed by Edwin Ivey, it was a charming and irregularly planned two story English residence sheltered by various pitched and gabled roofs. Its simple stucco exterior was punctuated by a prominent Tudor arched portal with raised mouldings and a rhythmic repetition of multipaned window groups.

159

Emma Baillargeon. DSB

Architect Charles Platt's rendering
of the east elevation of Thomas and
Emma Stimson residence, 1924.
SMC

Right, Formal entrance drive and
grass circle in front of Thomas
Stimson residence, ca. 1930.
MOHAI

Rendering of an alternate treatment
for the entrance door and balconied
second floor window, which was
finally selected,1924. SMC

children.[2] She and her siblings were educated at eastern convents and boarding schools. Emma was sent to St. Loretto Abbey in Toronto at age six in 1892. She returned to Seattle after college graduation in 1908. If she had been interested in design at that young age, she would have seen and admired the R. D. Merrill house in Seattle, a splendid neoclassical building with formal gardens that Charles Platt designed in 1909.

Baillargeon had done quite well in business. His wife, heir to a portion of the Collins estate, had also brought substantial monies to the family, which Baillargeon invested for his children's benefit by purchasing the southeast corner of Fifth Avenue and Pike Street (the site of the Logan Building).

Both Thomas and Emma were familiar with irregularly planned English-styled homes, having grown up in them. Emma dreamed of a classical, symmetrically planned house reminiscent of the Italian and French country homes she had visited on her trips to Europe. Her scrapbooks for several years prior to the building of the house were full of photographs of houses and rooms, primarily continental, showing her evolving interest in and attention to period architecture and decoration.

In 1923, Emma wrote to one of the best known practitioners of this style, Charles A. Platt, asking him to design her house on the 16.5 acres she and Thomas owned in the Highlands.[3] He declined because of age and distance. However, one day he telephoned her from Chicago, saying that as he had gone that far, he would continue on to Seattle. He visited twice and designed a two-and-one-half story home and a one-story garage.

Platt had attended the National Academy of Design and the Arts Students League in the 1870s and studied and travelled in Europe during the 1880s, where he was attracted to Italian Renaissance villas and the importance of integrating building and landscape. Though he failed to gain entry to the Ecole des Beaux Arts in 1883, by the 1890s he was designing small homes and gardens for himself and friends in New Hampshire. By the turn of the century, he was beginning to generate a client list for large formal country homes and landscape, following in the footsteps of McKim Mead and White and Carriére and Hastings. Platt saw the

---

2. One of her sisters, Abbie Ann, married Harold Stimson, son of Frederick Stimson.

3. Interview with Frank Bayley, son of Frances Ann Stimson and grandson of Emma Baillargeon Stimson. The original 16.5 acres has, through subsequent sales, been reduced to 7.6 acres.

villa as the appropriate precedent for the American house and increasingly pursued the translation of Renaissance forms to modern needs.[4]

Platt had been trained as a landscape painter and took great efforts to respond to the importance of views into the landscape when siting a building. He preferred to set the house high upon a hill, the ground falling away from it with some abruptness, and the landscaped surroundings simple so as not to compete with the architecture or the view. Platt often withheld the view for which the site was chosen until the visitor entered the house, at which point an axial vista opened from the entrance to the distant landscape.[5]

Platt believed that symmetry or its effect was essential to a beautiful building. Central sections of his principal elevations were almost always symmetrical and any lateral wings balanced if not identical. When a plan required wings of different sizes or only one wing, Platt used landscape to conceal this imbalance. The entrance or stairhall was always centered in the main elevation and received careful attention as the focus of circulation in the house.

Main Entrance

4. Keith N. Morgan, *Charles A. Platt The Artist as Architect* (Cambridge Mass: MIT Press, 1985), 46.

5. Keith N. Morgan, *Charles A. Platt The Artist as Architect*, 80.

Back view of house , showing stairs
and lawn, ca. 1930. MOHAI

Garden sculpture ordered for the
niche below the rear terrace. SMC

Dining room of the Platt designed
residence. (TB)

The Stimson house epitomized Platt's design principles. It bore similarities to continental
country houses and to English Georgian architecture, particularly in its restrained ornament, the
symmetry of the facade, the use of stone quoins set
into the plain stucco exterior walls, and the inclu-
sion of bullseye windows in the principal facade.
The gable roof was covered with slate and had
numerous dormers. The main approach to the
house was down a driveway from the main road
to a circle of meticulously trimmed grass lawn.
The principal entrance was quite simple. The rear
side of the house, which faced the view of water
and mountains, was more appealing. French doors
led to a landscaped brick terrace. The terrain of the
property, with a lawn sloping downward to the
west, permitted the rear of the house to have an
elegant double curved staircase with wrought
iron railings and a niche with statuary.

The interior of the house was as restrained
and dignified as the exterior. The entrance and stair hall were of
panelled and painted woodwork and the stairway wrapped around
and ascended past a curving panelled wall. The drawing room also
had panelled painted walls with acanthus leaf cornicing and classically ornamented fireplace surrounds and mantel. Ornate crystal
chandeliers and wall sconces, large mirrors, a grand piano, tapes-
tries, oriental carpets, and upholstered or slipcovered sofas and
chairs combined to create a handsome and comfortable place for

conversation. Subsequent to his presenting her with plans for the house, Emma corresponded with Platt about procuring furniture and furnishings for the house through him during his European travels, which accounted for some of the choice antiques throughout the house. Platt even provided the scenic landscape murals in the drawing room, which he painted at an earlier date.[6]

The painted, panelled dining room had fern-patterned draperies, a Chinese blue carpet with floral border, and a mahogany dining room set in the Empire style with ormulu fittings and marble counters. The library and den panelling were a light mahogany. A painting of an ancient Roman scene was installed above the library fireplace mantel.

---

6. The Platt Office Papers in the Charles A. Platt Collection, Avery Architectural Library, Columbia University lists the project as follows: Thomas D. Stimson residence, Olympic Drive, the Highlands Country house, garden, casino, swimming pool and garage. Ds. 1923; garden 1927. $150,319.31 CAPC Avery. IN 1929. The four landscape panels are not listed in the Avery project list. The house was variously remodeled and enlarged in minor details by the Stimsons.

Living room, Thomas Stimson
residence, ca. 1930. TB

Stair hall, ca. 1930. TB

Library, Thomas Stimson residence, ca. 1930. TB

Clara Wing Stimson, C.W. Stimson, and Jane Stimson Miller at Brookwood , ca. 1926. SMC

It didn't take long—1928—before Emma's brother, J. Cebert Baillargeon, a banker, relocated to "Faires Home" in the Highlands. He purchased the gambrel roofed colonial of Anna Hoge and her husband, Hamilton Rolfe.

Willard Stimson's son and C.D.'s nephew, C.W (Cully) had married Clara Wing and they had settled in Portland. In 1913, he organized the Stimson Timber Company at Belfair, Mason County. That justified a move to Seattle and the Highlands seemed the perfect spot. Later, he became president of the Stimson Timber Company in Seattle. He was responsible for building the company's trade with South America and Hawaii.

Brookwood, the English-styled C.W. Stimson home, was designed in 1924 by Seattle architect Edwin J. Ivey based on some of the ideas and plans that Clara Stimson had been collecting for a number of years. Born in Seattle in 1883, Ivey had attended the University of Pennsylvania and returned to Seattle, where he established a successful residential practice. It may have been his work for the Downeys that brought him to the attention of C.W. Stimson. Completed in 1926, the residence was located at the eastern edge of a 4.6 acre park. It was a two-story brick building measuring 87' by 33' with a garage attached to the house at a 45-degree angle. Its hipped roof was punctuated by dormers and chimneys. Its medieval details included a pointed arch portal and arcade and leaded glass windows. The Wing family crest was placed above the entrance door.[7]

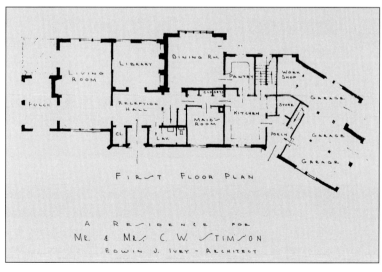

C.W. Stimson residence exterior ca. 1929 MOHAI

Edwin Ivey's first floor plan for the C.W. Stimson residence. UW

---

7. John R. Ross, *Clara Wing Stimson: A Reminiscence* (Portland:John Ross and Associates, 1984), 7.

**The formal garden and pond at
Greenway as completed. MOHAI**

When Dorothy Stimson and A. Scott Bullitt married in May, 1918, they moved to Bullitt's native Louisville, Kentucky, where he practiced law. But in 1919, Bullitt was given the opportunity to work for the Judge Advocate General, and they moved to Washington, D.C. When they returned to Seattle in 1920, he joined the C.D. Stimson Company. His interest in politics led eventually to leadership of the Democratic Party in the Pacific Northwest. In 1926, he was a nominee for the U.S. Senate.

When lumberman Chester H. White died and his 4.7-acre property adjoining Norcliffe to the south became available, the couple purchased it and made it their own, calling it "Greenway." The two-story Colonial Revival-styled dwelling had been designed by architect Carl Gould and built in 1916. It featured the gabled roof, shuttered multipaned windows, and central pillared entrance with pediment typical of the style. Several plans had been proposed for the gardens by the Olmsted Brothers, and while the formal Italian Renaissance design, with a central pool and a site divided into four quadrants, was executed, the Whites had not chosen to build the handsome balusters, walkways, and trellises suggested in a rendering prepared by the firm's local representative.

The Bullitts went to the original architect, Carl Gould, to design a sunroom addition in 1924. In the spring of 1927, they engaged architect Edwin J. Ivey. His introduction to the Bullitts may have been through the Downeys or C.W. Stimson, whose houses he had designed, or through Dorothy's brother and sister-in-law, for whom he had designed a children's playhouse on the Norcliffe property in 1921. In 1927, Ivey was also in the process of designing a residence nearby for one of C.D. Stimson's closest associates, Horace Henry.

For Greenway, Ivey designed two additions for an estimated cost of $12,500. In a June 2, 1927, letter, Scott Bullitt reiterated the agreement they had made in an earlier meeting: he agreed to pay him a flat fee of $850 to prepare plans and specifications and indicated that he would not be required to superintend the contractor's work. The additions, done with the same materials and scale of detail, seem as though they are a part of the original house.

The Bullitts had bought their household goods from a Louisville furniture firm when they were on the east coast and brought it with them when they moved back to Seattle. In March

1927, with remodelling being discussed, Mrs. Bullitt contacted with Raymond C. Gould Fine Arts, a Los Angeles furnishings house, to provide new mahogany dining and living room furniture and wall hangings in the English style. The inventory listed bronze lamps; mirrors; English biscuit jars, glass, and silver,;and a glass vase for the piano to accessorize the rooms. The sum came to $5,770. Gould suggested that "this is a nice start in re-arranging your rooms, however considerable more charm could be added to the Living Room if you cared at this time to spend a little more money." By Sept. 19, 1927, a revised list that included furnishing the library as well with suitable damasks, brocades, and velvets brought the total to nearly $10,000. An additional furnishings bill for over $1,000 was paid to the Cheeswright Studios, Inc., in Pasadena.

By 1929 then, the western edge of the Highlands abutting Olympic Drive housed C.D. and Harriet, son Thomas D. and Emma, Emma's brother J. Cebert Baillargeon and her cousin Emma Collins and her husband Archibald Downey, daughter Dorothy and A. Scott Bullitt, and nephew C.W. and Clara Wing. The Stimsons were "at home." C.D. died on the night of Aug. 29, 1929, at the age of 72,

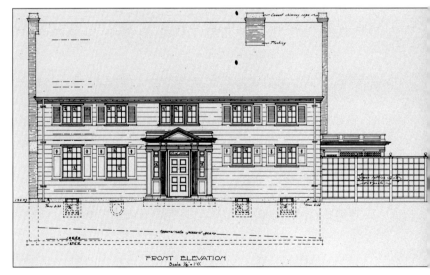

FRONT ELEVATION

Olmsted rendered landscape plan for pool and pergolas at Greenway. **DSB**

Front elevation of the original residence designed by Carl Gould. UW

Dorothy Stimson and A. Scott Bullitt on their wedding day (May 16, 1918) at Norcliffe. From left to right: Charles W. Stimson, Dorothy Terry Bullitt, Keith Bullitt, Jane Somervell, Scott and Dorothy, Thomas Stimson, Emma Baillargeon Stimson, Frederick Struve, Florence Williams Jones. DSB

Front drive and entrance, Greenway ca. 1928, DSB

content in the knowledge that he had done his best to provide his family with financial security through his many business enterprises and the buildings that he had built or encouraged in the Northwest. But more than that, he had—as his father before him—encouraged high values, a respect for honest work, and an appreciation for the importance of family.

Among the many newspaper accounts of his life and accomplishments, the *Seattle Post-Intelligencer* pinpointed Stimson's importance as builder and the significance of his projects to the growth of the city.

Seattle mourns not merely a millionaire and a pioneer, but a builder, one of the foremost of the brotherhood that razed hills, filled tideflats and reared spired temples of business to replace the virgin forests that vanished in the path of progress. Most of us are born to obscurity. Some flash to meteoric fame. C.D. Stimson and the builders of his brotherhood fall in neither classification. With the vision of leadership they had also the canny knowledge that the Seattle of the future was too big to be a one-man job. So they worked, not singly, but in groups, and not for a day, but for the long vista of the unmeasured future. No single building is a miracle, but the transformation of midtown Seattle, under the leadership of C.D. Stimson and his associates, came close to the miraculous.[8]

8. "C.D. Stimson 1857-1929," *Seattle Post-Intelligencer*, August 31, 1929, HH.

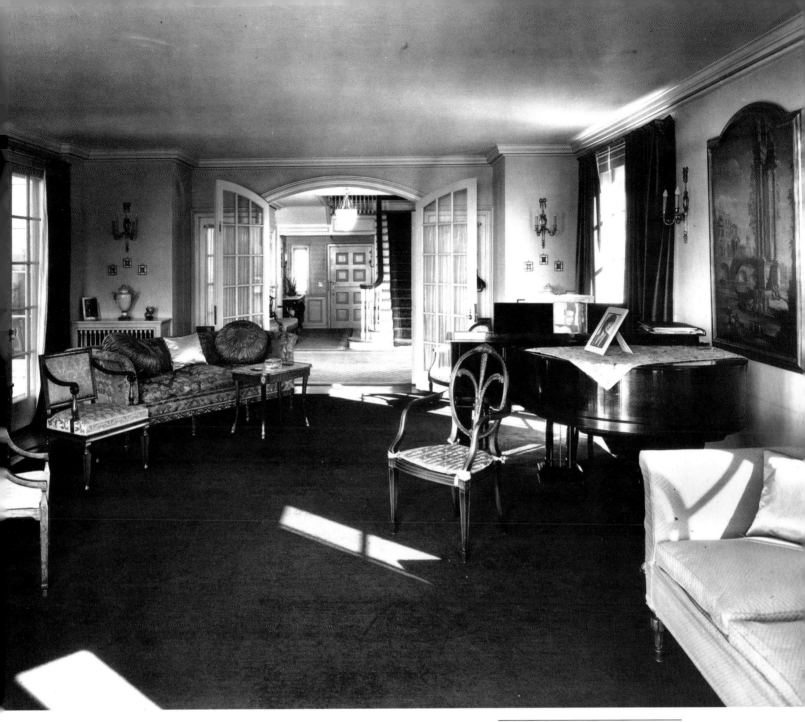

Living room at Greenway, ca. 1928.
View to front hall. DSB

Dining room at Greenway, ca. 1928
DSB

The library ca. 1928. DSB

The Bullitts, from left to right: A.
Scott, Harriet, Stimson, Dorothy,
and Priscilla. DSB

EPILOGUE

Architect R.C. Reamer's office had just completed some substantial commercial projects by 1929, among them the Bellingham Hotel, the Mount Baker Theatre, the Seattle Times Building, the Great Northern and the 1411 Fourth Avenue buildings. The Fox Theatre in Spokane and several smaller jobs were in the office. He must have thought it somewhat of a diversion when C.D. Stimson asked him to design a playhouse for his grandson, Stimson, on the Greenway property. There was already a tradition in the family of a children's retreat—Edwin Ivey had designed an idyllic English cottage in miniature at Norcliffe. It was fondly remembered by their children, grandchildren, nieces and nephews, some of whose names were inscribed on the walls of the building.

The Reamer designed playhouse at Greenway. SMC

The Reamer project was less a playhouse than a place where a boy would learn the vocational skills thought by grandfather C.D. to be essential for a man to know. Architecturally, the house was interesting because it was so "vernacular"—very much a pioneer cabin made of sawn lumber with simple windows and doors and a small porch. How out of place it was among the sophisticated Italian villas, English and French country homes, and American Colonial residences that surrounded it in the Highlands. Indeed, it was a place where young Stimson could have contemplated his roots, back to his grandfather and great grandfather whose first Michigan house had been almost as rudimentary. In its simplicity, it would remind the next generation that the Stimsons were self-made, that they, like their great-grandfather, Thomas Douglas and his sons, should not expect to be pampered but only to be supported in hard work and good deeds.

It was also, for all its plainness, a symbol of the built legacy that had its roots in simple Midwest cabins and farmhouses, was then nurtured by the French and English medieval and Renaissance castles of Big Rapids, Chicago, Los Angeles and Seattle, and reached maturity in the villas and country houses of the Highlands and in the broader vision of providing places for work, for entertainment and recreation, and for a satisfactory lifestyle on Puget Sound. It was a legacy that the children were heir to and to which they could aspire.

INDEX

Photo Credits / Abbreviations